Marginality

NO LIMITS

NO LIMITS

Edited by Costica Bradatan

The most important questions in life haunt us with a sense of boundlessness: there is no one right way to think about them or an exclusive place to look for answers. Philosophers and prophets, poets and scholars, scientists and artists—all are right in their quest for clarity and meaning. We care about these issues not simply in themselves but for ourselves—for us. To make sense of them is to understand who we are better. No Limits brings together creative thinkers who delight in the pleasure of intellectual hunting, wherever the hunt may take them and whatever critical boundaries they have to trample as they go. And in so doing they prove that such searching is not just rewarding but also transformative. There are no limits to knowledge and self-knowledge—just as there are none to self-fashioning.

Connection: How Technology Can Make Us Better Humans,
    Dan Turello
Contemplation: The Movements of the Soul, Kevin Hart
Rapture, Christopher Hamilton
Storythinking: The New Science of Narrative Intelligence, Angus
    Fletcher
Taste: A Book of Small Bites, Jehanne Dubrow
*Self-Improvement: Technologies of the Soul in the Age of Artificial
    Intelligence,* Mark Coeckelbergh
Inwardness: An Outsider's Guide, Jonardon Ganeri
Touch: Recovering Our Most Vital Sense, Richard Kearney
Aimlessness, Tom Lutz
Intervolution: Smart Bodies Smart Things, Mark C. Taylor

Marginality

Jin Y. Park

SOLIDARITY AND THE FIGHT
FOR SOCIAL CHANGE

Columbia University Press
New York

Columbia University Press
Publishers Since 1893
New York   Chichester, West Sussex

Library of Congress Cataloging-in-Publication Data
Names: Park, Jin Y. author
Title: Marginality : solidarity and the fight for social change /
    Jin Y. Park.
Description: New York : Columbia University Press, [2025] |
    Series: No limits | Includes bibliographical references and index.
Identifiers: LCCN 2025016621 (print) | LCCN 2025016622 (ebook) |
    ISBN 9780231209366 hardback | ISBN 9780231209373 trade
    paperback | ISBN 9780231557900 ebook
Subjects: LCSH: Marginality, Social | Equality | Social change
Classification: LCC HM1136 .P385 2025 (print) | LCC HM1136 (ebook)

Cover design: Chang Jae Lee

GPSR Authorized Representative: Easy Access System Europe,
Mustamäe tee 50, 10621 Tallinn, Estonia, gpsr.requests@easproject
.com

Contents

Acknowledgments

This book emerged from countless conversations and encounters across continents and decades. I am deeply indebted to my colleagues, students, and fellow travelers whom I met on my life's journey in the United States, South Korea, Europe, and other parts of the world. Their probing questions and fresh perspectives helped shape these ideas. I am grateful to Costica Bradatan for including this work in the No Limits series. The anonymous reviewers' careful readings and thoughtful suggestions greatly improved this manuscript. I thank Wendy K. Lochner at Columbia University Press for her guidance and steadfast support throughout this project. I extend my appreciation to future readers who will spend time with this work. I look forward to engaging in dialogue with them.

Marginality

Introduction

An Invitation

How do we envision a better life when we find ourselves in disadvantaged positions, our lives seemingly shaped by forces beyond our control? Are those at the margins doomed to remain at the mercy of the center? Our world is growing increasingly polarized, the center becoming smaller yet more powerful while the margins expand. Those at the margins struggle to find their way forward as paths to hope narrow. Could a twist of fate reverse this relationship, placing the margin at the center and vice versa? Would such a reversal resolve our society's divisions, or would it simply create new ones? The margin is not a homogeneous group characterized merely by disadvantage, and the center is not simply defined by power, wealth, and privilege. Neither the margin nor the center is fixed. What kind of reflection, theory, and action are needed to transform this stratified society and move toward a more equitable future in which all of our lives are valued and appreciated?

This book invites us to consider these questions by focusing on the meaning and values of the margin. The categories by which people are marginalized are numerous: skin color, gender, sexual orientation, region of origin, religious affiliation, financial status, and ontological position have all been used to subjugate individuals or groups to disadvantaged positions. In addition, the center's excessive power can suddenly thrust individuals who never considered themselves marginalized into positions of powerlessness and hopelessness. While no one desires to be on the margin, careful reflection reveals that almost everyone experiences marginalization in some way. As such, the key question becomes: Should marginality define identity solely in negative terms, or can we reimagine it as a productive force for improving our lives?

This book engages with the question of marginality through concrete examples drawn from life experiences. Each chapter begins with a brief episode from my past, all of which date back decades. They are like scenes from old movies—brief moments that have lingered with me over time. The images I describe remain as vivid to me as if they happened recently. I began to wonder why these moments stood out in my memory, even though they were not significant milestones like birthdays, graduations, or first dates. In hindsight, I realize that the sadness, shock, confusion, and discomfort I felt in those moments settled inside me like sediment, gradually transforming into philosophical language. These emotions found expression in the major themes of my scholarship as my academic career unfolded. The raw faces of those moments, feelings, and questions were concealed behind more technical discourse in my publications. They were shielded by the logic and conventions of scholarly writing, but the intense emotions I experienced seemed to demand a more explicit expression and interpretation. They had been silenced; but in this book, I finally give them a voice.

Writing a book on marginality based on my personal experiences also carries several implications about how we generate meaning and value in our lives and what it means to do philosophy. Some might argue that philosophy and life stories should remain separate. The conventional wisdom in philosophy as an academic discipline holds that logos and mythos, or truth and stories, should belong to distinct realms. A story is seen as subjective, while truth is viewed as universal and should not be muddled with the contingencies of individual experiences. But if we do not draw from our own daily experiences for material to create meaning and value in life, where should we find this meaning and value? Furthermore, we do not live merely as individuals; we live in community and in the world. Our experiences always occur within contexts, meaning that our existence has never been confined to personal or private realms. It unfolds within a web of communal existence, and our experiences carry meanings that extend beyond the limited scope of an individual's world. Moreover, when we think about community in our time, it is not limited to human groups. It also includes entities that humans often exclude in value-laden discourse, such as nonhuman animals, inanimate objects like rocks, trees, flowers, and oxygen, and our fellow machine beings, such as robots and other forms of AIs.

The idea that philosophy is inherently connected to our personal experiences, which are communal, also sheds light on what it means to do philosophy and who can be a philosopher. Many people view philosophy as an abstract subject that is disconnected from daily life. The twentieth-century Korean philosopher Pak Ch'iu (1909–1949), however, had a different perspective. He argued that a philosopher is not someone special, but rather someone capable of "hearing with their 'heart' the demand of reality—the cry that reality is shouting at us, asking for the resolution of the problems of our time."[1] Pak characterizes the core activity of philosophy as praxis—action grounded in theory and directed toward goals. In this sense, philosophers are distinguished by their responses to the reality they encounter. When a philosopher confronts a reality that does not align with their vision of life, they strive to bring about change. Praxis, or the action taken to transform reality, can take various forms, from street protests and activism to shifting our perspectives and altering how we treat others in daily life.

The expression "public philosophy" has recently emerged in academic discourse. The idea contrasts with academic philosophy, which often becomes highly technical in its arguments. Public philosophy, on the other hand, seeks to engage the public, both in terms of content and accessibility. But if we define philosophy the way Pak did—in relation to life experiences and the production of meaning—philosophy at its core cannot be anything but public philosophy. In public philosophy, narrating life stories plays a significant role. Storytelling, or narration, is one of the oldest practices that humans have used to make sense of our experiences. The act of giving meaning by telling and retelling our experiences is what I refer to as narrative philosophy. Theories often rely on technical concepts in order to gain legitimacy from experts, and the same holds true in academic philosophy. Such a practice, however, places many groups of people in the position of having no language to express their experiences and values, since the experts' vocabularies and value systems are based on those who have privilege. Those who have historically been excluded from such privilege—such as non-Western individuals, women, and people of color—face challenges in presenting values and theories that are rooted in their own experiences. The power dynamics involved in such philosophical practices highlight the importance of approaching philosophy through the lens of narrative philosophy. Everyone has life experiences, yet not everyone's vocabulary is recognized as a legitimate philosophical one. By giving voice to my daily experiences, this book serves as an exercise in decoding them and connecting them to the meaning and value we seek in our lives.

In writing this book, I explore various forms of marginality and their effects, shedding light on the pervasiveness of marginalization in our thoughts and life experiences through concrete examples. Despite the omnipresence of marginalization in society, I do not seek to lead the reader into a dystopian worldview but rather invite the reader to reconceptualize marginality and thus suggest that such a reorientation requires changes in how we think and how we relate to others and ourselves. In this sense, my aim is to reframe marginality as a tool for challenging the status quo, which often stigmatizes and disparages the margins, and to propose the power of the margin as a force for social change.

Marginality consists of five chapters that address: (1) various forms of marginality, (2) the logic of exclusion as the operational framework of marginalization, (3) violence as a key driver of the logic of exclusion, (4) the minority-against-minority strategy of marginalization, and (5) an invitation to reflexive engagement. The materials I used to develop these discussions include some Western philosophy, but they are primarily drawn from Eastern sources, Buddhism, South Korean literature, Asian American literature, and also African American literature and films. Some of these may be unfamiliar to many readers, but I believe that my choices align with the book's central theme: an exercise in expanding the scope of our social imagination and doing philosophy from the margins.

The topics I discuss are by no means exhaustive of all forms of marginality. There are many cases that I was unable to include, partly because of the limitations of my own experiences. My hope is that this book offers a framework through which we can think about the question of marginality, raise awareness of discrimination, and address the larger issue of how individuals create meaning and value at the margins while engaging in transformative change.

While I completed this book, some of the issues discussed here along with others related to its spirit reached a new threshold. The Supreme Court's decision to strike down *Roe v. Wade* in June 2022, which had protected women's reproductive rights, has resulted in a concerning decline in public health and a reduction in women's agency over their bodies and lives. In June 2023, the Supreme Court also ruled race-based affirmative action in college admissions unconstitutional, while students from underprivileged backgrounds continue to struggle to access quality education and find their place in a racist society. And American society has changed radically, which I briefly mention in the epilogue. These events make the issues discussed in *Marginality* even more urgent and relevant today.

My imagination is shaped by my personal experiences as an Asian in a West-centered world and an Asian American in a white-centered society, having lived in a nonnative country for more than thirty years and become a citizen of it. I have navigated life as a woman in a patriarchal world, and I have spent decades teaching non-Western philosophy in an academia dominated by Western philosophical traditions. There are many elements that can lead an individual to feel marginalized. Similarly, I believe that each person, regardless of their position on the spectrum between the margin and the center, has their own form of marginality that creates a sense of insecurity in their life. Our individual reactions to the insecurity induced by perceived marginality may vary; a person may avoid confronting the marginalized aspects of their life and instead highlight seemingly central and powerful aspects of themselves, or they may acknowledge and face their marginality. I believe that acknowledging and sharing our own marginality can help create a space where it can be transformed into a positive force for change, allowing communities to move forward.

1

Departure

A woman swallows her tears. The people around her seem to be in high spirits. Her niece, a fifth-grader standing beside her, is all smiles, dressed in red for her first international journey to visit her grandparents in the United States. After the trip, the niece will often tease her aunt, recalling how the adult had cried at the airport while she, the child, bravely endured her departure from home, leaving behind her parents and familiar surroundings.

That was true. Tears welled up, but not so much because the aunt felt sorrow about leaving what people called "the motherland," the place where she was born and had grown up. Nor was it because she had to say goodbye to her friends and leave all her memories behind. She might have felt, in a way, that she was being forced to leave. The gap between the life she had envisioned for herself and the prerequisites demanded by society to realize it seemed unbridgeable. She was a woman in a patriarchal society, from a middle-class background in a capitalist system, with no connections to anyone in power. She didn't even have an acquaintance in academia, business, politics, or any other field in a society where connections were essential for almost anything she hoped to achieve in her future.

When I think of the day I first left South Korea, these images from the airport still linger. To be an outsider in one's own community and to sense one's own invisibility not only makes one feel like a stranger in that society but also a stranger to oneself. The Bulgarian French feminist philosopher Julia Kristeva wrote, "The foreigner enters when the consciousness of my difference arises, and disappears when we all acknowledge ourselves as foreigners, unamenable to bonds and communities."[1] Many people may have experienced the first part of Kristeva's statement, but conceptualizing the second part does not prove as easy. What would it mean to recognize that everyone is a foreigner?

Feeling invisible makes one a foreigner—a stranger to oneself—as one's projected and perceived identity finds itself in limbo, without a stable anchor by which to claim one's identity. "The foreigner is a baroque person,"[2] Kristeva wrote, meaning that a foreigner is a person of "irregularity," much like irregularly shaped pearls—an image that, according to one theory, can be traced back within the etymology of the term "baroque." Irregularity presumes a regularity against which it can be defined. What defines the regular shape of a pearl? Who defines the regularity or standard by which to measure a person? For many, the word "baroque" has associations with the musical style of composers like Bach, Handel, and Vivaldi, whose works are recognized even by those with little knowledge of music. Why did these famed composers pursue irregularity? Can we, too, be irregularities and still occupy central positions in society, as these musicians do in the history of Western music? Does irregularity eventually become regularity as time passes? These questions bring us to a deeper tension between regularity and irregularity, much like the tension between the stranger and the native. Which is more visible, regularity or irregularity? A common-sense response to this question might be "irregularity," since things that are irregular are often seen as different. But visibility, or the act of being seen, is not always defined solely by visible appearance. In fact, a visible appearance, due to its difference, might make such irregularities invisible.

In the African American writer Ralph Ellison's *Invisible Man* (1947), the narrator begins his story by addressing his invisibility: "I am an invisible man. No, I am not a spook like those who haunted Edgar Allan Poe; nor am I one of your Hollywood-movie ectoplasms. I am a man of substance, of flesh and bone, fiber and liquids—and I might even be said to possess a mind. I am invisible, understand, simply because people refuse to see me."[3] As Ellison's narrator explains, invisibility is a constructed phenomenon. Physical invisibility occurs when the human capacity for vision fails to perceive the subtle existence of things, rendering them invisible. For example, molecules or atoms are too small to be detected by human eyes; but with the right instrument, scientists can detect their existence. The invisibility of molecules is produced by the limitations of human eyesight. Similarly, social invisibility arises from societal shortcomings. The invisibility of women in a patriarchal society, or of Black Americans in white-dominated American society, emerges from society's failure to recognize them for who they truly are.

DEPARTURE

The social invisibility of African Americans contrasts with the visibility of their physical features, such as the color of their skin and the texture of their hair. Similarly, the invisibility of women accompanies the conspicuousness of their physical bodies. Blackness is painfully visible, yet this visibility ironically leads to African American people being rendered invisible. In a patriarchal society, a woman's visibility paradoxically contributes to her invisibility. In American society, second- and third-generation Asian Americans, who were born and raised in the United States, are still often asked, "Where are you from?" The visibility of their appearance makes them perceived as foreigners in their own homeland. When the coronavirus hit the United States, these Asian Americans were subjected to insults fueled by fear, with phrases like "Go back to your home!" directed toward them in their own country. The question remains: Where are their homes?

Chinese Americans arrived in the United States in the mid-nineteenth century, followed by Japanese and Korean Americans. African Americans, however, have been in this land much longer: the first slave ship arrived in 1619. Yet in the twenty-first century, they continue to face challenges regarding their identity as Americans. Foreigners, strangers, women, African Americans, and Asian Americans all share a common experience: visible invisibility.

Existentialism, which developed within continental philosophy, offers profound insights into the experience of being a stranger. The sense of uncanniness that arises from our existence, whose fundamental meaning is often ambiguous, is central to creating a figure like Meursault in Albert Camus's *The Stranger* (*L'Étranger*, 1946), a work that brought Camus international fame and led to his Nobel

12

Prize in Literature in 1957. In the story, Meursault kills an Arab on the beach the day after his mother's death, justifying his action by claiming it was caused by the blinding sunlight.

In the context of the unending gun violence in American society, the story of a young man randomly killing someone on a beach due to an existential conundrum might not resonate as powerfully, even though it is intended to be read symbolically. But as the widespread fame of the book attests, the extreme incident Camus uses in *The Stranger* powerfully conveys the depth of human angst in confronting the reality of existence and realizing there is no inherent ultimate meaning in our lives.

Camus's fellow existentialist Jean-Paul Sartre summarized this situation with a simple sentence: "Existence precedes essence."[4] We are not born to fulfill a predetermined mission or to serve as part of a grand design within which our existence is situated. Instead, we are "thrown" into the world, and from there, we must construct meaning, if we choose to do so. An immediate reaction to this interpretation of our existence might hold that it presents a pessimistic view of life, emphasizing, as Sartre puts it, "a state of quietism and despair." Sartre addresses this criticism in his famous work *Existentialism Is a Humanism*, wherein he argues that the absence of foundational references to anchor values and actions in our lives should lead to freedom, not despair. This situation allows humans to define themselves and make their own choices, he contends, asserting, "Man is nothing other than what he makes of himself."[5] Humans are condemned to freedom, and it is up to them to shape their lives and find meaning, Sartre argues. In modern society, freedom is one of the most cherished values, especially within democratic societies. How can one be "condemned" to be free? We will return to this question shortly.

Another objection to the existentialist view that our lives are not part of any grand design with inherent value holds that it presents an atheistic approach to life. From a religious perspective, one might argue that if we believe in a creator, we should trust that the creator knows why we are here. But such a religious claim does not fundamentally alter the conundrum posed by existentialist philosophers. While the creator may have a plan for our lives and understand the reasons for our existence, this does not mean that human beings can access or comprehend the creator's intentions, especially given that the creator is ontologically different from us. The transcendental being is "wholly other," as the German theologian Rudolf Otto puts it. The gap between the transcendental being and human beings is not merely a matter of degree; it is qualitatively unbridgeable. Therefore, Søren Kierkegaard, whose existentialism does not deny the existence of God, argues that religious faith requires a leap, one that must be taken blindfolded.

Kierkegaard draws on the biblical story of Abraham and Isaac to illustrate this point. Abraham, a faithful servant of God, was granted his first son, Isaac, with his wife Sarah when he was a hundred years old. Then he received God's command to sacrifice his son. As a father, the idea of sacrificing a child is unimaginable, yet as a believer, such an incomprehensible action had to be carried out without question when commanded by God. Abraham, in his faith, was prepared to do just that.

Kierkegaard argues that, from a religious perspective, Abraham was a faithful man. But from an ethical standpoint, Abraham was hovering on the brink of becoming a murderer by committing parricide. In the end, God intervened and spared Isaac, and the common interpretation of the story often emphasizes God's mercy in doing so. The Bible does not mention Abraham's suffering or any doubt in his faith. Yet Kierkegaard shifts the focus away from God's mercy and instead highlights the absurdity and paradox that a person must endure on the path of sustaining faith. He invites the reader to imagine the profound suffering that Abraham must have experienced as he journeyed to the mountain, preparing to sacrifice his own son.

Kierkegaard defines Abraham's situation as "a teleological suspension of the ethical."[6] Although Abraham is a singular human being subject to the ethics of his society, in the biblical story, he also represents the universal figure who directly communicates with the absolute. As such, he must think and act according to both the universal and the absolute—which, however, is absurd because Abraham is, in fact, an individual human being who cannot help but endure extreme suffering at the thought of killing his own son. This paradox, this absurdity, defines the religious worldview, according to Kierkegaard. While God must have an intention and purpose for human beings' existence, that intention and purpose are not meant to be easily shared or understood by humans. Human beings are strangers in the world of the absolute, marginal beings within the spectrum of ontology. The struggle to find meaning and value in one's existence remains their task, with no guarantee of success.

The existentialist idea that "existence precedes essence," that beings are not born with a predefined essence or mission, bears a fundamental similarity to the philosophy of

Buddhism. Buddhism asserts that nothing in the world possesses a permanent or independent essence. Instead, things exist through interconnectedness, each contributing to and depending on the other. Thich Nhat Hanh (1926–2022), the Vietnamese monk who coined the term "engaged Buddhism," explains this idea of interconnectedness as follows: "If you are a poet, you will see clearly that there is a cloud floating in this sheet of paper. Without a cloud, there would be no rain; without rain, the trees cannot grow; and without trees, we cannot make paper. The cloud is essential for the paper to exist. If the cloud is not here, the sheet of paper cannot be here either."[7]

16

Through this reasoning, Thich Nhat Hanh suggests that we should understand "to be" as "to inter-be." We are not "beings" but "inter-beings." As he says, "Without a cloud, we cannot have paper, so we can say that the cloud and the sheet of paper inter-are." If we follow Thich Nhat Hanh's explanation, we can see our existence in terms of hyperlinks on the internet—each word leads to the next, which in turn leads to another. We may continue clicking the blue hyperlink in search of the ultimate word, the ultimate meaning, only to realize there is no final endpoint.

If existence precedes essence, and no beings in the world are born with predetermined missions, as existentialist philosophers argue, by what measure and through what process do we become strangers, foreigners, or marginalized beings? If beings do not exist as self-sufficient entities but are fundamentally "inter-beings," as Buddhism teaches, what causes the marginalization of certain individuals or groups among us, and what justifies the privilege of those of us at the center?

As we consider these questions, we recognize the differences between a stranger, a foreigner, and a marginalized being. The English term "stranger" derives from the Old French *estrange*, meaning foreign and, by extension, bizarre, whereas "foreigner" refers to a territorial boundary as a measure of difference. Whether qualitatively different (a stranger) or territorially different (a foreigner), both terms signify a departure from what is considered the norm. When this difference resonates within us, we become strangers to ourselves; an existential crisis may follow. The gap within our own selves, the sense of strangeness encountered in moments of uncertainty, creates an inner void. We find ourselves no longer at home within our own being. Existentialists describe this feeling as "uncanny," signifying moments of alienation from within as we feel disconnected from our own existence.

In *Nausea*, Sartre's existentialist novel, the main character, Antoine Roquentin, experiences nausea when he holds a pebble at the seashore. The sheer weight of the pebble's existence in his hand fills him with a repugnant discomfort: "I was going to throw that pebble, I looked at it, and then it all began: I felt that it existed. Then, after that, there were other Nauseas; from time to time, objects start existing in your hand."[8] At its core, nausea is a bodily response that occurs when the body's synchronized activities or coordination fail to function properly. Motion sickness, such as seasickness, happens when the body's movements are not properly communicated to the brain.

One might experience touching something that causes a sudden start, leading to an immediate withdrawal of the hand. As Roquentin observes, doorknobs or pebbles usually appear to us as mere objects, not as things with existence. But the moment we perceive an object as something more than just an object, our bodies react. When chopping beef, if for a brief moment, one feels the chunk of meat to be something other than just material for dinner, the relationship between the person and the object shifts. The body then reacts, attempting to redefine that relationship. Is the chunk of flesh on the chopping board merely food, or did it have life before it arrived there? When one realizes that both are true, the relationship with that chunk of flesh becomes elevated to a new level.

Sartre's rather amusing character in *Nausea* presents us with two contrasting interpretations of our existence. On one hand, for Roquentin, his encounter with pebbles marks an awakening to existence itself. Pebbles on the beach or doorknobs in our home usually evoke no specific response from us. They simply exist, and we take their presence for granted. Their "existence" is ignored, as we encounter them merely as "functional objects." Roquentin's nausea serves as a wake-up call challenging our taken-for-granted attitude in daily life that shapes how we encounter others. On the other hand, his nausea when holding a pebble or a doorknob points to the meaninglessness of their existence. They are not just functional objects—they *do* exist. But what does their existence mean? Like a pebble or a doorknob, Roquentin's own flesh lacks a foundational meaning.

The proposal to recognize the existential nature of a pebble or a doorknob might sound absurd or even counterintuitive, but the deeper meaning is not simply that these things exist. Rather, it is that we, too, exist without any preprogrammed essence. The sense that our own existence can be, and is, like an unrecognized pebble on the beach, or that our own flesh can be like a chunk of meat on the chopping block, demands that we realign the seemingly clear hierarchy of existence between a human being, an animal, and a pebble. This brings us back to Sartre's claim that existentialism is humanism, in the sense that, without a pregiven essence or a being to direct our existence, humans are free to construct the meaning of our own lives. This leads us to revisit the theme of freedom mentioned earlier, asking if freedom is an unconditionally positive element in our existence, or if it is possible that people might actually want to *escape* freedom, despite the constant demand for it, revealing the irony inherent in the existential reality of human beings.

For most people, the grandeur of freedom is accompanied by a sense of loss and a feeling of being lost. Human beings typically seek freedom and will even die for it. At the same time, as Erich Fromm eloquently articulated in *Escape from Freedom* (1941), humans do not always embrace or use freedom constructively. Instead of using freedom to creatively shape their lives, people often seek refuge in structures that provide roles or positions that give meaning to their existence. This voluntary abandonment of freedom is pervasive in our time. People may live under the illusion that they are free, when in reality, they are becoming slaves to consumerism in a capitalist system, or to the political mechanisms of the totalitarian regime that they are allowing to control them.

Fromm used Hitler and National Socialism as examples of people's willing surrender of their own freedom and their fear of taking full responsibility for their lives. The German American political theorist Hannah Arendt's account of Nazi officer Adolf Eichmann's testimony during his trial, as described in her *Eichmann in Jerusalem: A Report on the Banality of Evil* (1963), illustrates this point well. Eichmann, a man with no distinctive career, family background, or particular talent, found that Hitler's National Socialism gave meaning to his life, and he believed that he was a valued member of that organization.

After the defeat of Germany, Eichmann managed to escape and lived in Buenos Aires under a false identity. He was eventually captured through an international operation, as depicted in the movie *Operation Finale* (2018), and later put on trial in Israel. When tried for his role in Nazi atrocities, including the "Final Solution" to eliminate the Jewish people, he defended himself by claiming that he had been a law-abiding member of society, and what he had done during the Nazi era was legal according to the laws of the Third Reich.

Arendt writes that May 8, 1945, the official date of Germany's defeat, was a pivotal day for Eichmann because "thenceforward he would have to live without being a member of something or other."[9] In Eichmann's own words, "I sensed I would have to live a leaderless and difficult individual life; I would receive no directives from anybody, no orders or commands would any longer be issued to me, and no pertinent ordinances would be there to consult."[10] People's willingness to give up their freedom, even without being aware of it, makes totalitarianism possible. To be condemned to freedom, to make our own decisions, is more than just burdensome. It is horrifying, as it forces us to confront the emptiness of our existence. Escape from freedom, from making decisions, means avoiding self-reflection, without which our sense of self is reduced to a name without meaning. And without a sense of self, we cannot truly consider others.

The Korean Buddhist nun and thinker Kim Iryŏp (1896–1971) wrote that after she became a Buddhist nun, three observations led to shocking realizations about the nature of the self and freedom in her time: first, she realized that "I had lost my own self"; second, "the entire world consists of people who have lost their selves"; and third, people were unaware of this condition, still believing themselves to be intelligent.[11] Iryŏp's diagnosis that most people in her time had lost themselves stemmed from her observation that people fail to fully exercise their freedom, instead indulging in a system that constrains it.

What Fromm defined as an "escape from freedom," Iryŏp described as a "loss of self," because without the active construction of the self through free choice, a person's self is not truly their own but rather a hostage of the system in which the individual invests. In this sense, freedom is inevitably tied to power, the power to exercise our individual freedom and the power to take responsibility for our individual actions. This brings us back to our discussion of strangers.

Being a stranger does not necessarily equate to being on the margins. Power is not always the determining factor in whether an individual is perceived as a stranger. Marginality is primarily an indication of power dynamics. The term "stranger" also carries a sense of power imbalance, but a stranger is not necessarily someone on the margins of the power structure, because foreigners and strangers are not invariably subordinated to the native. When Europeans arrived in the Americas, they were strangers to the natives.

They were not on the margins, however. Soon, they controlled the natives and transformed them into colonial subjects. When Europeans invaded Africa, they were also foreigners, but they quickly conquered the natives and became the landowners. The histories of empires are, in many ways, the stories of strangers subjugating natives through the force of their power. The Roman Empire, the Mongol Empire, the Ottoman Empire, and the colonial and imperialist movements of modern history all testify to the power of the stranger.

There are more specific terms for foreigners who arrive from outside, such as migrants, refugees, immigrants, and expatriates. The United States is fundamentally a nation of immigrants. Except for Indigenous peoples of North America, all Americans have either moved to this country from elsewhere or are descended from those who did. Immigration, however, is no longer an issue confined to countries like the United States. South Korea, once touted as a nation that had held a homogenous ethnic group for millennia, has recently witnessed an influx of migrants arriving as workers or brides, alongside individuals coming to the country for business or study.

Refugees are perhaps the most marginalized group of migrants. "Contemporary reflection on refugees begins with the shadow of the Holocaust," asserts Joseph H. Carens, a political scientist.[12] Since then, the world has witnessed multiple waves of refugees caused by war, internal conflict, and other events, such as Cuban refugees in the 1960s and 1970s, Vietnamese refugees in the 1970s, and more recently, Syrian, Afghan, and Ukrainian refugees. The United Nations' 1948 Universal Declaration of Human Rights recognizes "the right of persons to seek asylum from persecution in another country." In 1951, the UN also issued the Convention and Protocol Relating to the Status of Refugees.

People often ask: Who has the obligation to care for refugees? Why should a democratic nation feel compelled to accept refugees? The answers to these questions link closely to the issues of marginality that we are considering. The strangers characterized as migrants, refugees, immigrants, and expatriates are all subject to the differentiation between the inside and the outside.

Kristeva once described the contrast between the outside and the inside as follows: "*Elsewhere* versus the origin and even *nowhere* versus the roots."[13] The concept of origin or roots suggests a value that humans attach to a person or thing that can be traced back to the past. The practice of valuing ancestry and recording family lineage suggests that while the present may offer limited information for evaluating a person, the past can serve as a guarantor or enhancer of their value. For those who have traveled far from their birthplace, such a backstop does not exist. They are viewed like floating dandelions. To immigrants, people might say, "Whoever your father, your mother, or your ancestors might have been, we don't know them, and you don't want them, since you have left them." What would compel such migrants, beings with no past, to put down roots in a new place? Is it even possible?

The logic of negating the past of migrants is implicitly tied to the concept of "naturalization," a process that migrants must undergo to become permanent members of a nation-state. As the political scientist Benedict Anderson discusses in *Imagined Communities* (1983), the terminology and concept of naturalization assumes that the

23

nation-state is a natural form of community, and that citizenship within it serves to secure and confirm a natural form of existence.[14] In the book, Anderson asks what makes people willing to die for their nations. This question is crucial to him because, as the title suggests, he views a nation as an "imagined" community, not a natural one. The members of this community never meet all the others, nor do they expect to. Further, it is imagined as a limited community, as no nation seeks to bring the entire world's population into its citizenry. It is also imagined as sovereign, having emerged from a challenge to the power of a monarchy, even though the locus and scope of the nation-state's sovereignty remain unclear. Finally, it is imagined as a community, even though inequity and exploitation are widespread within it.[15] What kind of community is a nation-state that systematically enforces and sustains the inequality of its members? Yet naturalization reinforces the naturalness—and thus, the legitimacy—of the nation-state.

The nature of a nation-state as an imagined community has become clearer recently, as many countries, including the United States, South Korea, and several European nations, suffer from a bipolar division between the extreme right and extreme left, or conservatives and liberals. While a division based on social and political agendas and beliefs might be natural in human communities, the extreme polarization that leads to violence, such as the January 6th riot in the United States or the recent attack on a courthouse in South Korea, vilifies those who do not share the same ideas and attempts to violently damage the lives of their opponents.

Much like territoriality, the body, which is our individual territory, has been a source of marginalization. Since time immemorial, the female body has been treated as "impure," a frequent justification for the subordination of women in patriarchal societies. This impurity is often explained in terms of menstruation: women must expel blood every month to cleanse their bodies; the undeniable irony of this claim is that without women's menstruation, no human being would exist.

Buddhism asserts that no beings possess a preinvested essence and that all things exist through webs of interconnectedness. If Buddhism is to remain true to this fundamental tenet, there is no reason why women should be treated as inferior to men within its tradition or be disqualified from enlightenment. Yet the history of Buddhism, like that of most major world religions and philosophies, has been patriarchal in nature.

The discrepancy between Buddhism's claim of the non-existence of unchanging or independent essences and the inferior position of women in the tradition is evident in a group of Buddhist texts known as "body transformation" literature. In the Lotus Sutra, a major scripture of Mahāyāna Buddhism, an eight-year-old dragon girl asserts that she has attained awakening. Śāriputra, a disciple of the Buddha renowned for his wisdom, derides her by saying, "The body of a woman is filthy and not a vassal of the Law [Buddhist teaching]. How can you attain supreme awakening?"[16] At that moment, the dragon girl transforms her body into a male one. Does this story prove that a woman can attain awakening in a female body, or does it suggest that women must transform their bodies into male ones to attain awakening? Debates on this issue abound.

A story in the Vimalakīrti Sutra, another key text in Mahāyāna Buddhism, adds further complexity to the issue. In this story, Śāriputra again scoffs at a goddess who claims to have attained awakening, pointing out the unfit nature of a woman's body for enlightenment. This time, the goddess transforms her body into a male one and changes Śāriputra's body into a female one, demonstrating the insubstantiality of the body. Whether these texts actually helped promote women's position in Buddhism historically is unclear. Not until the late twentieth century, when feminist Buddhist scholars began interpreting these texts in the context of gender inequality, would they be understood to support gender justice. When it comes to discrimination and marginalization, rational thinking—often credited as a major characteristic of human beings, especially since the Enlightenment—tends to fall short.

Territorialization and the controlling power that accompanies it also manifest in the realm of ideas. Philosophy has long claimed to be searching for truth and wisdom, asserting that truth should be objective and universal. But are objectivity and universality region-specific qualities? Can they be particular to gender or race? The history of academic philosophy shows that it has maintained its power by centralizing a white, Western worldview while excluding the thought traditions of other parts of the world and presenting them as unfit for addressing wisdom, truth, values, and the meaning of our existence.

A quick look at some modern Western thinkers provides examples that support this point. The German philosopher G. W. F. Hegel (1770–1831) believed that history

progresses from the East to the West, with the East representing the childhood of human history, characterized by
naiveté and immaturity, whereas the West symbolizes its
culmination. Since the people of the East had yet to reach
maturity, the gods they worshiped were also inferior to
their Western counterparts. Hegel placed Eastern religions
such as Buddhism and Confucianism at the early stages of
the evolution of religion in human history, asserting that
the final consummation occurred with Christianity.[17]

For Edmund Husserl (1859–1938), an Austrian German
philosopher known for founding the philosophical school
of phenomenology, only Europe could save the civilization
of the world, because "only in the Greeks do we have a universal ('cosmological') life-interest in the essentially new
form of a purely 'theoretical' attitude."[18] Asians, in contrast, had only universal but mythical attitudes in their
thinking, Husserl argued. Therefore, for Husserl, the
Europeanization of the world was not only justifiable but
inevitable, as it was necessary to preserve the world's civilization.[19] As Kwok-ying Lau, a scholar of intercultural philosophy, summarized it, for Husserl, "Europe alone [is] the
bearer of the 'absolute meaning' of the future development
of the entire human civilization."[20]

The claim that only the West, particularly Europe, can
serve as the source of wisdom and truth clearly emerges
in the philosophy curriculum of today's higher education,
which is dominated by Western philosophers and philosophies, as well as male thinkers, while non-Western thought
traditions are largely ignored. As Bryan Van Norden, a
scholar of Chinese philosophy, points out, among the top
fifty PhD-granting universities, "only four have a member
of their regular faculty who teaches Chinese philosophy."[21]

27

Van Norden's article was published in 2016, and while changes may have occurred since then, I doubt there have been any drastic changes in this regard.

The effects of the systematic exclusion of non-Western thought traditions and nonmale thinkers extend beyond philosophy education. This practice introduces, reinforces, and perpetuates a West-centered worldview among young people, rendering more than half of the world's thought traditions irrelevant to our understanding of life and society. Further, it fails to provide opportunities to engage with diverse perspectives in a rapidly globalizing world. While Plato, Aristotle, Descartes, Kant, Hegel, and Heidegger dominate the stage of philosophy, the marginalized philosophies from around the world—Asian philosophy, African and African diaspora philosophy, Latin American philosophy, women's philosophy, and many more—wait in the wings for an opportunity for recognition.

Marginalization occurs through the center's power to define the values, meaning, and normalcy of our existence. Hannah Arendt defined power as a collection of capacities, stating that "power corresponds to the human ability not just to act but to act in concert." We may be accustomed to expressions like "I have the power to do" this or that, but power cannot be individual. Arendt explains, "When we say of somebody that he is 'in power,' we actually refer to his being empowered by a certain number of people to act in their name."[22] We witness this phenomenon in political rallies; elections in a democratic society serve as a demonstration of this understanding of power.

Arendt's insight also helps us reconsider the relationship between marginalization and power. Like power, marginalization is not an individual situation. While marginalization can be directed at a single person, what upholds it is the group that supports the discrimination against that person. Power is structural, but its structure is not like that of a building. A building can crumble and collapse due to cracks in its structure, but fissures and crevices in the structure of power are difficult to pinpoint, and more often than not, power survives them. We can say that the structure of a building is mechanical, whereas the structure of power is organic. An individual or group representing power may be removed, but what sustained their power often remains. Hitler was removed, and his power came to an end, but what enabled him to hold power endured: anti-Semitism and racism continue to sustain themselves.

I have presented shades of marginality along a spectrum stretching from the philosophical and existential, as seen in the figures of Camus and Sartre, to the concrete, as experienced by migrants. This scale can also be described as ranging from the most existential to the most political. In between, we encounter a mix of existential, cultural, social, and political issues such as gender, race, social class, philosophy curriculum, and worldview. None of these issues is solely philosophical or political. The mosaic presentation of the groups, expressions, and identities at the margins reveals how ideas of hierarchy and power dynamics permeate our everyday lives, from our vocabularies and thought systems to our politics and their execution.

Despite the bleakness that human existence may seem to take on as we become aware of the diverse forms of marginalization that infiltrate our lives, the goal of this book is not to dwell on the darker aspects of our existence. Neither existentialism, Buddhism, nor any of the thinkers I have referenced in this chapter encourage us to be pessimistic about life. Instead, they all call for action: to engage in the creation of meaning and values and to take responsibility as the owners of our lives and as members of the community of beings. The demand for action also serves to restore agency to marginalized people.

In Buddhism, action, or karma, is a structural foundation of the world and existence. In Sanskrit, the word "karma" literally means "action." Every moment, we act. Actions occur through the combination of various elements, which Buddhism refers to as causes and conditions. The same action can have vastly different effects depending on the conditions in which it takes place. For example, if I add a spoonful of salt to my cup of tea, my tea will become unmistakably salty. But if I add the same amount of salt to the Pacific Ocean, no human palate would be sensitive enough to detect the change. The key points are twofold: all actions have consequences, but these consequences are not easily calculable because they unfold through the permutations of the conditions in which the actions occur.

Being aware of the nature of our actions is the first step toward liberation in Buddhism. Buddhist teachings on karma emphasize the agency of the actor and highlight the actor's responsibility for their actions. Failing to recognize the nature of our actions leads to suffering. The Buddha asserted that the elimination of suffering was the goal of his teachings. From an existentialist perspective, awareness of the nature of one's existence should lead to engagement with reality, providing a means to exercise one's freedom.

In concluding our review of the various forms of marginality, let us return to a fundamental question of our topic: How does marginality arise if one is not born with an essence? African American writer James Baldwin (1924–1987) may offer an important perspective in answering this question. When Baldwin died in 1987, he was working on a piece titled *Remember This House*, which focused on three figures: Medgar Evers, Malcolm X, and Martin Luther King Jr. All were assassinated: Evers in 1963, Malcolm X in 1965, and King in 1968. The unpublished manuscript, along with other writings and transcripts of Baldwin's public talks, appears in Raoul Peck's documentary film *I Am Not Your Negro* (2016), which concludes with a 1963 PBS interview with Baldwin from the series *Negro and the American Promise*.[23] Baldwin ends the interview by saying, "What white people have to do is try and find out in their own hearts why it was necessary to have a 'nigger' in the first place, because I'm not a nigger, I'm a man. But if you think I'm a nigger, it means you need him. . . . If I'm not the nigger here and you invented him—you, the white people, invented him—then you've got to find out why. And the future of the country depends on that, whether or not it is able to ask that question."[24]

31

In other words, the burden of proof should not rest on African Americans to demonstrate that they are human beings like white people, but on the white people who define other human beings in such an inhumane way. Similarly, the burden of proof does not lie with women to demonstrate that they are as capable as men; rather, the patriarchal society that has constructed women with specific characteristics and roles and that continues to demean them should question why it has been necessary to create such a stratified treatment of human beings. A person is not inherently a marginal being but is made marginal by

the society that defines and treats a person as if their existence holds only a marginal meaning (if any).

We can ask the same question that Baldwin posed about
those at the margins or about marginality itself. If the center
created the margins, it must have had a reason to do so: Is
there a discernible logic used consistently in the creation
and maintenance of marginalization? A consideration of
this question is now in order.

2

Exclusion

The candidates sat in a large ballroom, like a herd of animals about to be sold. Waiting to be summoned by interviewers from the universities each had applied to made them uncomfortable. Before entering in the waiting room, most of them likely felt good about themselves—certainly the woman did—for making it to the semifinal stages of the job search. But sitting anonymously, a group of nameless candidates preoccupied by their chances of being hired, that sense of achievement evaporated, replaced by fear and uncertainty. Their prospective employers, faculty members with full-time jobs, could exert whatever power they wished.

"Mr. Park," a male professor called out.

Could that be me? A Mr.? I'm not a Mr., the woman thought. But she didn't see anyone else with a Korean face, and Park is one of the most common Korean last names. Sheepishly, she raised her hand. The professor noticed and justified himself by saying, "Oh, I'm not familiar with the genders of foreign names." No apology. Her Korean first name is, in fact, gender neutral. *This doesn't look good,* she thought.

Thinking back on that interview, I still wonder how the professor decided on my gender when he couldn't tell by my first name. He could have simply called out my full name without using "Mr.," or he could have called me "Dr." since I had already earned my PhD by that time. Instead, the professor chose "Mr. Park."

I cannot say for certain whether the gender trouble I encountered even before the job interview started had any bearing on my not getting the position. But I can't help thinking that I was excluded from the job before the interview even began, before I had a chance to demonstrate my qualifications. A woman was out; a man should have been there.

Nowadays, semifinalist interviews in academic job searches are often conducted online, using various meeting platforms, a shift that occurred after the pandemic made people resigned to virtual meetings. In these settings, the candidate's face is visible, which might have mitigated the gender trouble I experienced in the in-person interview. But gender isn't just binary, and to avoid such issues, many people now include pronoun designations after their screen names: she, he, they, and so on.

Some might think that connecting a search committee member's ignorant assumption of a candidate's gender to that candidate's not getting the job is an example of exaggerating or overthinking of a trivial issue. It is very possible, however, that the human mind operates in a convoluted way. Moreover, the sense of loss or even inadequacy that women experience when confronted with the notion that the default should be male is not insignificant.

I strongly suspect that I am not the only female job candidate who has encountered a version of this scenario in a job interview.

A philosophy professor once studied the relationship between gender, ethnicity, and the value of scholarly works by examining the gender and ethnicity of the 267 most-cited authors born in 1900 and after in the *Stanford Encyclopedia of Philosophy*, one of the most prestigious encyclopedias in the field. Of the 50 most-cited authors, only 2 percent were female, and none were members of minority ethnicities. Among the 100 most-cited, 7 percent were female and 1 percent were minorities. Among the 267 most-cited, 10 percent were female and 3 percent were minorities.[1] One might simply respond to this survey result by confirming that white males are conducting more valuable research, which is why people reference their publications more frequently. That may be true, but should we really be convinced that, for over a hundred years, only white males have produced valuable research in philosophy? If we reflect on this question, we are confronted with a different perspective on our scholarly activities and how they are evaluated by the academic community, which can be understood as follows.

The simple fact that a scholar is male or white often increases the value and authenticity of the claims and research presented in their scholarly publications. Works by women and scholars from minority groups are frequently ignored or are not considered to be valuable research worthy of attention. Their contributions are excluded from the competition for academic recognition. How much are readers' intentions involved in this phenomenon? It's difficult to say that anyone intentionally decides to tie a scholarly work's value and validity to gender or ethnicity. But unconventional wisdom repeatedly claims that when a woman presents an idea in a meeting, participants simply listen and move on, whereas when a man presents a similar idea, it is praised as groundbreaking. Bias is not skin-deep, and neither are the various forms of exclusion in our society. They are intricately intertwined with the structural injustices that have become deeply embedded in our society.

In spring 1994, Donald Kagan, the dean of Yale College, gave a moving speech to the first-year students about the centrality of Western values, urging them to defend these values against its critics. According to Kagan, those who criticize Western society, pointing to its history of "slavery, imperialism, racial prejudice, addiction to war, and its exclusion of women and people not of the white race from its rights and privileges,"[2] diminish its grand values. His speech moved some audience members so deeply that Yale received a $20 million donation from a Texas oil family to hire professors to teach Western civilization. The *New York Times* published an excerpt of the speech alongside a response by Henry Louis Gates Jr., a renowned African American professor, who asked, "Whose Culture Is It Anyway?" Gates argued that the common culture of the West that Kagan urged people to defend was, in fact, "Anglo-American regional culture, masking itself as universal."[3] For Louis, American culture cannot be reduced to a homogeneous white Anglo-Saxon Protestant (WASP) culture. If the culture of a society is understood as a product of its members, the diversity of American society must be acknowledged, with Anglo-American culture being just one of many different cultures present.

As Gates clearly demonstrated in that opinion piece, what the center claims to be universal is, in fact, a "universalization of regional values," and its status as universal is made possible by the exclusion of other cultures, values, and groups, which are demoted as inferior and unworthy of attention. The center justifies its dominant position and its claim to universal values that everyone should follow in various forms, including rituals that celebrate its victories. The Fourth of July is one such ritual, in which American society reaffirms its values by celebrating independence from colonial Britain and promoting the ideals of equality and freedom. But this celebration encounters a grim reality when race is factored into the equation.

In a speech delivered on July 4, 1852, titled "What to the Slave is the Fourth of July?," Frederick Douglass (1817 [1818?]–1895), a former slave who became a statesman and social reformer, asked the gathered assembly, "What have I, or those I represent, to do with your national independence? Are the great principles of political freedom and of natural justice, embodied in that Declaration of Independence, extended to us [former slaves]?"[4] The Fourth of July that white Americans celebrate "brought stripes and death" to Black Americans. Douglass thus declares, "This Fourth of July is *yours*, not *mine. You* may *rejoice, I* must mourn."[5]

More than 150 years after Douglass's speech, the racism that divides the meaning of the Fourth of July into two opposing narratives endures. The American celebration of Independence Day is made possible by the exclusion of those who have been subjected to slavery, poverty, and discrimination. Similarly, American society's celebration of Thanksgiving serves as a marker of the exclusion of Indigenous peoples of North America, whose way of life was permanently destroyed when white Americans invaded their lands.

Exclusion from society equals expendability, suggesting that the excluded group will not have significant impact on the functioning or survival of the society. The center argues that, while these excluded groups on the margins may contribute to society, their contributions are not regarded as essential to the society's existence, prosperity, or sustainability. But we know that a society does not exclusively rely on those who hold power and wealth. The contribution of slaves to the American economy in the pre-Emancipation period is a prime example of this. Similarly, the roles of migrant workers in the American economy have been repeatedly denied by those who seek to punish and expel undocumented individuals and migrants.

A community's sustainability is not measured solely by its economic capacity. A society that values only a certain group of people not only risks its own sustainability but also faces the danger of a totalitarian mentality that endorses certain ideas exclusively and vilifies those who do not support them. In such a community, the prevailing ideas are typically those advanced by those in positions of authority. The more rigid a society becomes, the more people will uncritically follow ideas that define their values through the exclusion of others. As strict and punitive declarations of ideas and proposals come to dominate rather than conversation, creativity will wane.

On the surface, those on the margins are the first victims of such a government and leadership, including migrants, asylum seekers, economically disadvantaged people living below the poverty line, women, people of color, sexual minorities, and more. At a deeper level, the entire society—including those who seem to prosper by supporting the totalitarian path—will have to pay the price: either through the loss of their values and humane relationships, or by depriving younger generations of the opportunity to learn about and experience a world that grows through the creative coexistence of diverse views, ideas, values, and preferences for how to lead a life without causing suffering or damaging others and oneself. This inevitably leads us to rethink what it means to be human or who might be classified as disposable and by what measure.

One way to consider this question is by thinking about humans' relationship with nonhuman beings, namely machines. In our digital age, with the intricate connection of our daily activities to digital devices, a new dimension of ethical questions regarding human relationships with others can be introduced into a discussion of the disposability of the margins. In this context, we can ask a seemingly simple and naive question: Which is more valuable, a human being or a machine? The answer may seem straightforward. "Human beings, of course," we would respond. But what if we modify the question and ask: How are humans and machines related in the lifestyle of the twenty-first century?

Human beings tend to think of themselves as the creators of machines like computers, smartphones, and various forms of AI. The logic follows that humans are the masters of the machines they created. With the exponential advance of digital technology in recent years, people's encounters with machines have become a regular part of daily life, even though most people might not think of their relationship with a laptop or Siri in these terms. The concept of a machine has also evolved significantly with the advent of digital technology. Machines are no longer just trains, airplanes, refrigerators, and production equipment. Today's machines, especially in the form of humanoids, perform a wide range of functions. They can serve as caretakers in senior citizens' facilities, take on the role of a boyfriend or girlfriend, or even work as a monk in a monastery. This shift raises new questions about the nature of human-machine relationships, the roles that machines can play in our lives, and what this means for our understanding of both humanity and technology.

Machines need to be constantly replaced in this world of rapidly advancing technology, so they are considered disposable. But when does the disposability of machines raise a question of ethics for us humans? What does the disposability of machines have in common with that of humans? We might not think much about the disposability of a smartphone when updating it, but what about the AIs and robots that are already assisting humans in roles like serving meals at a restaurant or running errands? During a recent trip to South Korea, I encountered a robot working as part of the hotel housekeeping team. I requested extra packets of coffee grounds, and they were delivered by an AI robot that knocked on my hotel room door, handed me the packets, and then returned to its "base station." Should the AIs or robots who deliver coffee make us pause and think differently about whether those machines are disposable as well?

In the 1980s, the science fiction series *Star Trek* addressed this issue with serious thought. In episode 9 of season 2 of *Star Trek: The Next Generation*, titled "The Measure of a Man," a scientist wants to dismantle and transfer

Lt. Commander Data, an android, with the intention of creating many more androids with similar capabilities, as Data is one of only two existing androids with such advanced capacity. If Data undergoes the reassembly process, he risks memory loss and other side effects, so he requests not to be transferred. The scientist, frustrated by the android's refusal, argues that Mr. Data, as a machine, is property of the Starfleet ship; therefore, the machine has no right to make decisions for itself and must comply with the request. Captain Picard, however, maintains that Lt. Commander Data is not merely a machine but a Starfleet member with the right to make decisions for himself. Picard's objection leads to a trial to determine whether Lt. Commander Data is simply a thing, a piece of Starfleet property, or a being with the same right to self-determination as human beings—hence the title of the episode, "The Measure of a Man." The episode raises the central question: What qualities and qualifications are necessary to define a human as human, as opposed to another type of being, such as a machine?

Indeed, how can humanity be measured? The episode's argument reaches its peak when Picard engages in a conversation with a Starfleet member who compares the disposability of an AI being to the disposability of human beings in the practice of slavery. Slaves were not considered human beings and therefore were traded and treated as disposable. One might consider it overthinking to connect the disposability of humanoid robots to that of enslaved human beings. But are they really that distant from each other in terms of the logic that justifies their disposability? Have humans not treated their fellow human beings as inferior and thus disposable for the benefit of those with the power to control them? The question now is not only whether a machine should be given rights, but how humans' relationships with others—be they human beings, other living beings, machines, or even inanimate objects—will shape how humans live in the world and protect the values essential to their existence. By using this logic regarding humans' relationships with themselves and others and acknowledging the horror of the practice of disposability, Picard wins the trial, and Lt. Commander Data, an android, is granted the right to make decisions.

Captain Picard's defense of Data using humans' relations with other humans echoes the sentiments of an essay from premodern Korea titled "Eulogy for a Needle," written in the nineteenth-century by a woman known only as Lady Yu. As with many female writers in the premodern period, little is known about her, except for the assumption that she must have come from an aristocratic family, given that she was literate. According to the essay, she was widowed and childless. She took to needlework as more than a chore, viewing it as a meaningful occupation for her otherwise lonely life. She recounts that one of her in-laws brought her a pack of needles from Beijing, which she shared with her family, keeping only one for her daily work. Then, when the needle broke during use, she was heartbroken. Lady Yu expresses her grief over the "demise" of the needle so deeply that she concludes the essay by saying, "Even though you are a thing, if you are not ignorant of my feelings, I wish we could meet again in the next life and reconnect our relationship of living together."[6] Since this piece was written by a woman and needlework was considered a feminine task in the premodern period, the essay has often been interpreted and taught as reflecting women's lives. But the essay is not just about women's lives in premodern society; it is also about relationships.

For Lady Yu, the needle must have held more significance than a laptop or a smartphone does in our time. She formed a companionship with the needle through her daily use, and when it suddenly broke, she grieved as if for the death of a companion. We might not feel this way when a laptop or a smartphone breaks down, partly because they are considered replaceable. We can buy a new one at any time. Replaceability implies disposability, whether the object being replaced is a machine like a smartphone or a human being like a contingent worker. When they are broken or no longer needed, they can be replaced or removed from their positions.

Judith Butler defined "grievability" as a measure of the value of a being in her book *The Force of Nonviolence*. When a being is lost, that loss should be grieved. This seemingly commonsense understanding of death or loss, however, does not reflect the reality of our existence. As Butler argues, not only are not all lost lives grieved, but the level of grief for each lost life is not the same. Mourning is an act of recognizing the meaning and value of the lives of those who have passed, with grief playing a crucial role in that process. It is an acknowledgment of the irreversibility of the loss and, consequently, the unreplicability of the being who disappears from the mourner's world. Through mourning, we come to terms with the unique existence of the departed, understanding that their absence cannot be replaced or undone. When an individual or group is considered disposable, the loss of their lives does not receive an appropriate level of grief.

The funeral ceremonies and mourning processes that have existed for millennia across various human cultures are not merely about the afterlife. Whether the ceremony involves burying the dead in the best possible place according to geomancy, as in Confucian tradition, or cremation, as in Buddhism or Hinduism, these rituals serve to honor the being who has just departed from existence. The living mourn because the lives of the dead continue to hold meaning for those who remain. Funeral rituals and the expression of grief are testimonies to the value we place on beings who are no longer with us, and as such they assist the living in sustaining and protecting the meaning of existence and values.

Lady Yu's mourning and grief over the demise of her needle reveal the value she placed on that relationship—the connection she formed with the needle and the meaning that this connection held in her life, even though the needle was an insentient object. Similarly, Captain Picard in *Star Trek* defends Lt. Commander Data, an android, by arguing that the logic used to deny Data his right to make decisions for himself has also been employed in denying the rights of certain groups of people throughout history.

We should note, however, that the distinction between humans and nonhumans, or between the sentient and the insentient, is not at the core of exclusionary actions. If the logic holds that humans are more valuable than nonhumans, or that the sentient have a higher intrinsic value than the insentient, then members of the same group should at least be treated equally. But this has not been the case in most human societies. Once a hierarchical categorization is established, it multiplies. Humans and nonhumans are placed on a hierarchical scale; among humans, males and females are ranked; among males, white males and nonwhite males are measured vertically, and the hierarchical categorization continues. By excluding groups with less power in terms of gender, race, social class, economic status, and so on, the center consolidates its privilege and universalizes its values as objective norms for all beings. In reality, however, these are the local values of a specific group.

In this reflection on the center and the margin and the logic of exclusion that facilitates such divisions, the institution of higher education in the United States can be viewed ironically: it teaches students to destabilize and challenge the problem of the center's exclusion of the margin, while the university itself perpetuates the same dynamic. In recent years, more college and university faculty and staff members have considered or gone through the process of unionizing.[7] According to one report, "From January 1, 2013, to December 31, 2019, there were a total of 118 newly certified or recognized faculty collective bargaining units in the United States."[8] Graduate student workers are also unionizing at an unprecedented rate. These developments are signs that both faculty and students are increasingly marginalized in US higher education. So who, then, is at the center of higher education?

The hiring trends in US higher education from 1976 to 2005 show that the number of full-time nonfaculty professionals (i.e., high-level administrators) increased by 281 percent; at the same time, the number of full-time tenured/tenure-track faculty only grew by 17 percent. Additionally, the number of full-time nontenure-track faculty increased by 223 percent and the amount of part-time faculty increased by 214 percent. In other words, the number of tenured/tenure-line faculty barely grew, while contingent faculty, including nontenure-line teaching positions and part-time teaching positions, saw significant increases.[9] Outpacing all of these faculty positions were those of high-level administrators. The erosion of tenure-track positions and the increasing number of contingent faculty mean that job security for faculty members is disappearing. Once faculty members find themselves in contingent positions, their ability to challenge the undesirable practices and compensation gap within the university diminishes.

Adjunct faculty pay has remained largely unchanged for at least twenty years, leaving many of them hovering near the poverty line; meanwhile, some university presidents earn million-dollar salaries.[10] As a newspaper opinion piece points out, how can faculty members be expected to teach diversity, inclusion, and truth when they themselves live below the poverty line? And even for tenure-track faculty, the gender gap in compensation remains evident. According to the American Association of University Professors' "Annual Report on the Economic Status of the Profession, 2022–2023," female professors earn only 82.3 percent of what their male counterparts make.[11]

More and more universities are being run by professional administrators who treat universities like corporations, with faculty members increasingly excluded, both from governance and salary equity. In essence, faculty members are becoming marginalized within their own institutions. We might argue that in a modern capitalist society like the United States, for a university to survive, its leaders must be knowledgeable and skilled in management and fundraising. Although this idea is gaining traction today, it overlooks the foundational role that higher education plays in society. The political scientist Benjamin Ginsberg described it this way in *The Fall of the Faculty: The Rise of the All-Administrative University and Why It Matters* (2011): "Controlled by its faculty, the university is capable of producing not only new knowledge but new visions of society. The university can be a subversive institution in the best sense of that word. . . . Controlled by administrators, the university can never be more than . . . a knowledge factory [that meets the needs of] established institutions in the public and private sectors."[12]

Universities need funds to operate, but they are not corporations with the sole goal of generating profits. The fact that a university has a nonacademic president does not mean that faculty should be excluded from decision-making. But the erosion of shared governance is increasingly common in American higher education. The marginalization of faculty inevitably leads to their dissatisfaction, which has damaging effects on students' education. The bloat of high-level administrators whose compensation far exceeds that of faculty members has been a major cause of the rising costs of college education in the United States. This has resulted in a generation of young people either starting their careers with enormous student-loan debts or giving up on higher education altogether. A recent *New York Times Magazine* article argued that a society whose young people view a college education as a gamble in cost-benefit calculations is likely to lose competitiveness in the global market—and American society is facing that risk today.[13]

The gap between the theory of diversity, equity, and inclusion (DEI) and its reality is not limited to the faculty level. Students from minority groups also encounter this gap. Anthony Jack, a professor of education, described the practice of "structural exclusion" in US higher education in his book *The Privileged Poor: How Elite Colleges Are Failing Disadvantaged Students* (2019). In the 1970s, universities adopted policies of equal opportunity, which considered minority status as a factor in admissions. In recent years, some Ivy League universities have adopted a zero-burden financial aid policy, offering aid that does not need to be paid back. The goal is to provide financially underprivileged and underrepresented students with the opportunity to attend these schools. The practice also contributes to a more diverse student body. With annual tuition and housing costs exceeding $60,000 at many elite institutions, this may be the only way for students from low-income families to access the educations offered by these prestigious universities.

This good intention, however, is proving to be insufficient. The logic of exclusion cannot be ameliorated or eliminated with a single offer of free tuition and housing, no matter how generous that is. What the French sociologist and philosopher Pierre Bourdieu calls "cultural capital" cannot be created overnight.[14] In discussing the structural problem and the marginalization of underprivileged students, Bourdieu uses this term to refer to the sum of an individual's social assets, such as family background, lifestyle, and other factors. For example, a student from a well-off family that regularly vacationed abroad, dined out, visited theaters and museums, wore brand-name clothes, and had relatives holding professional positions with extensive networks would have far more social capital than a student who is the first in their family to attend college.

A first-generation college student rarely has many resources to draw on to navigate college life or understand what to expect in the classroom. They might feel awkward in various social settings in college and struggle to network. Their lack of exposure to fine dining or brand-name clothes could make it difficult for them to engage in certain common conversations. The structural exclusion they experienced growing up follows them onto campus even if their tuition is paid for. When universities tout their achievements in diversity, equity, and inclusion, they often highlight the numbers of incoming students of color, women, or members of underprivileged groups. But they are less eager to say how they support these students once they are on campus, living and learning alongside students who grew up with distinct privileges.

The logic of exclusion is applied preemptively to those who are excluded. In most cases, a person does not choose their gender, race, social class, or family, and the exclusion occurs even before those subjected to it make any statement or contest. The individual is preemptively excluded. Bourdieu uses the term "unexamined exclusion" to describe what I refer to as preemptive exclusion. When people are evaluated based on the group they belong to rather than on their own merit, unexamined exclusion is already operating in the form of what we call "discrimination."

The Marxist concept of capital focuses on the economic context of the individual, whereas Bourdieu's theory of social capital demonstrates that the individual's economic situation does not exist in a vacuum. It is shaped by a social and cultural milieu, and like material inheritances, socio-cultural conditions are passed down through cultural reproduction by the privileged. Those who do not share this privilege remain marginalized even when some financial resources are provided to them.

Using his concept of cultural capital, Bourdieu empha-sizes that the current educational system functions by reproducing and reinforcing the dominant culture, which is the culture of the privileged. In this sense, the premodern inheritance-based system of privilege persists in modern democratic society, despite the ostensible goal of the moder-nity project to dismantle the system. The claim of a discon-tinuity of privilege, both economic and cultural, between the premodern and modern periods, in fact, reveals how much remains unresolved.

Diversity, equity, and inclusion have evolved into ethical mandates in our society, beginning in the late 1990s and more actively through the early 2000s and into the mid-2020s. These principles came to extend across various sec-tors, including the federal government, business, and higher education. The growing emphasis on DEI reflected a broader societal shift toward addressing systemic inequalities and promoting fairness in all sectors.[15] Institu-tions of higher education have taken part in this trend, cre-ating offices for dealing with DEI and emphasizing the diversity of faculty and student bodies. Many institutions take pride in their achievements, showcasing the percent-ages of people of color among newly hired faculty mem-bers, or the proportion of nonwhite students. We should not underestimate these efforts and their results. But are these institutions truly practicing diversity, equity, and inclusion when their administrative structures operate in a discriminatory manner, and salary inequities have persisted for decades?

The Korean novel *A Dwarf Launches a Little Ball* (1978) illustrates the despair of people who suffer from intergenerational inequality, which traps them in marginal lives as factory workers deprived of education—the only means of escaping the snare of poverty and a humiliation. *Dwarf* tells the story of a lower-income family in Seoul in the 1970s, a period when South Korea was industrializing rapidly. The father is depicted physically as a dwarf, and it is not difficult to read symbolism into this, especially considering that disability studies had yet to develop in South Korea at the time. The family has one daughter and two sons. In the story, they receive an eviction notice because their house was built illegally, and the city is planning to demolish illegal housing in the region to make way for new apartment buildings. Gentrification is taking place under the guise of modernization. The government offers the residents money for the demolition of their house and the right to purchase a unit in the new apartment building. But the price of the new unit is more than double what they will be paid, leaving them with no hope of staying.

The three children all had to give up education at the middle school level as a result of financial difficulties. In South Korea, free elementary education has been available since 1959, but free middle school education was offered only in remote regions, and not until around 1985. It was only in 2005 that all regions of the country began to provide free middle school education. But even with "free education," students still had to pay fees, even at the elementary school level and long after 1959.

Both brothers understand the importance of education for escaping a life of poverty. As they say, their society is "primitive to a shocking degree" in the way it is divided between those who are educated and those who are not. Yet despite this awareness, education is not easy to obtain for those on the margins of society, like the dwarf's children. They are forced to work in a factory to support their family. To make matters worse, when the brothers demand improvements to their terrible working conditions, they are fired.

One of the sons reflects, "Those 'educated' people who read *Hamlet* and shed tears over Mozart's music perhaps have lost the capability to weep over the desperate suffering of their neighbors."[16] This observation reveals the stark reality of the gap between those with education, cultural capital, and privilege and those who live on the margins of society. The lack of understanding or concern among the privileged for the disenfranchised only deepens the misery of the latter. In this sense, cultural capital is as ruthless as economic capital, and the two go hand in hand.

In the printing factory, while typesetting documents related to an old serf-trading record, one of the sons realizes that his family's predicament is not a recent development. It has a long history, like the family mentioned in the trading record, marked by generations of suffering at the bottom of society:

> Serfdom was abolished during the time of my grandfather's father. At the time, my great-grandparents were not aware of it. Much later, when they learned about the emancipation, their reaction was "Please do not throw us out." Grandfather was different. He tried to break out of the

traditional customs. His old master gave him a house and some land. But it was no use. Grandfather was less ignorant than his father. Up until great-grandfather's generation, one could benefit from ancestors' experience, but in grandfather's time that experience provided no help. Grandfather had neither education nor experience. He lost his house and the land.[17]

Emancipation from serfdom alone will not enable people who have suffered for generations under inhumane treatment to suddenly stand independently. Even though families were provided with houses and land, their lack of accumulated knowledge—cultural capital—made it almost impossible for newly liberated people to compete with families who had owned houses and land for generations and had the know-how to manage them. Without such inherited financial and cultural capital, marginalized people like the dwarf's family must overcome intergenerational deficiencies, something that is not easily done.

So how should someone respond to an unequal reality, especially while still in a disadvantageous, marginal position? I will return to the story of the dwarf's family and explore how they responded to the seemingly insurmountable barrier of inequity and the logic that excluded them. Before doing so, I introduce another case of exclusion that led to a new mode of philosophizing.

The twentieth-century French philosopher Jacques Derrida (1930–2004) once revealed that his philosophy, known as deconstruction, was rooted in his experience of exclusion as a child. Derrida was born and raised in Algeria until he moved to Paris at age nineteen to pursue his studies. When he was around eleven, a school official came to his classroom and told him, "You are going to go home, my little friend, your parents will get a note."[18] Derrida related, "At that moment I understood nothing, but since?" As an eleven-year-old boy being expelled from his school, Derrida might not have been able to make a direct connection between his situation and anti-Semitism. He also did not likely understand that it was the French—his own government—not the Germans, who expelled him from school because he was Jewish.

Immediately after the incident, however, he found himself fully exposed to anti-Semitism: "The first few months after my expulsion was a very bad time; I had begun to experience anti-Semitism outside, in the streets, in my circle of friends, my old playmates who treated me like a 'dirty Jew' and wouldn't talk to me anymore."[19] The experience of being expelled and this unexamined exclusion evolved into Derrida's philosophy: he tried to create a new system of understanding, one that challenges and destabilizes the center while also examining the complex relationship between the center and the margin, as well as the center's grip on the margin.

Despite the pervasiveness of the dualism between the center and the margin—those who expel and those who are expelled—nothing in life is simply dualistic. The experience and trauma of exclusion can cultivate a desire for nonbelonging, as one tries to preemptively eliminate the possibility of being excluded. The logic is that not belonging to any group can prevent exclusion. The fear of the others who expelled an individual from the group (and who might do so again), the humiliation of encountering the negation of one's existence, and the powerlessness to defend one's life against such negation, push the excluded person to self-alienation. This alienation manifests as exile to the realm of oneself, away from those dreadful others. But the trauma of being expelled does not completely extinguish the desire for belonging. Instead, the expelled person seeks a bit of light leaking through a narrow crevice, signaling even a tiny possibility of still being accepted by the center. And if a person finds that crevice and attempts to squeeze through, acceptance will require a compromise. A "bad girl" can become a "good girl" by conforming to society's expectations for how a girl should behave. The temptation to do so never disappears.

The world has long been patriarchal, and the exclusion of women does not lead them to completely exclude themselves from patriarchal society. American society has been racist from its inception, but that does not lead people of color to leave the United States or refrain from coming to the United States. Is this because people believe that change is possible? That may be the case, but the dream of a new world might not be the only motivation for remaining in a world where they experience exclusion. Is it because withdrawing completely from a racist, patriarchal, and stratified society is not an option? To exist means to exist within a certain society, and at this juncture of history, the society that refuses to accept the marginalized person may be the only one available.

Or is it because, much as one can criticize and challenge the power of the center, a desire to be at the center also lurks in the heart of the expelled soul? Wouldn't it be ironic to criticize the center while still thinking that being a part of the center would not be completely loathsome? Is the desire to be at the center the same as the desire not to be at the margin? Or is the desire to be included different from the desire to be at the center? Is there a way for the center and the margin to intermingle? Are the center and the margins fixed, as they are mostly understood to be, or are they in a more mutually dependent relationship? To put it differently, the division between the center and the margin is not one-dimensional. There can be multiple layers to what constitutes the center and the margin in a person's life, which in turn influence their decisions about what makes life bearable and what counts as a central value worth protecting, regardless of their position in life.

Reflecting on the experience of being expelled from school, Derrida said that he felt it necessary to find "new categories" that would interrupt the center's claim to value by allowing an understanding of identities as mutually dependent. Derrida explains this new approach to identity employing "trace" and "différance," which Hugh J. Silverman, a scholar of continental philosophy, identified as deconstructive operators. In Derrida's philosophy, *différance* indicates that an identity is made possible by its difference from other identities, not because of any intrinsic nature of a being. In this framework, other identities remain as traces within a given identity. The alphabet letter *b*, for example, is *b* not because it possesses any inherent *b*-ness, an innate essence of *b*, but rather because of its difference from other letters of the alphabet in the English linguistic structure.

A *b* is not an *a*, nor a *c*, nor a *d*, and so on to *z*. Within *b* the other letters exist as traces, since without the other twenty-five letters, *b* cannot function as *b*. Understanding *trace* and *différance* in the context of this discussion of the center and the margin reveals the relational identities of the two. The center cannot exist without the margin, and the center's identity is defined by the existence of the margin. Through the marginalization of those who are not at the center, the center sustains its identity and consolidates its power.

The center might not feel threatened by this argument of relational identity, as it will continue to legitimize and demand the value of its identity. But the margin can and should be empowered by this logic, given that people on the margins of society are not there because the margin is defined by any intrinsic marginality but because of the center's logic, which is based on the exclusion of others. As we discussed at the end of the first chapter, with James Baldwin's words, white America constantly places Black Americans on the margins of society, but those who are placed on the margins by the center do not have margin-ness in their existence or value other than what is imposed on them.

Would the center listen to this claim of the interdependence of the center and the margin? Perhaps not, except as a political gesture. If someone is at the center and has privilege, would they give it up so willingly? I doubt it. But those on the margins should care about this logic. The "should" here is not necessarily related to moral and ethical obligation, however. Dominant Western moral theories and ethical imperatives have assumed that humans are rational beings with a sense of obligation. This assumption has been shown to not align perfectly with human reality, as evidenced by imperialism, colonialism, and the continued violence in the world. The image of the human being as rational and holding a deep sense of obligation was particularly prominent in modern Western philosophy, but history has revealed a far more troubling picture of human existence. History might not refute the human capacity to create a morally responsible society, but the claim of human rationality and the imperative of obligation have at least proven inefficient.

In lieu of the ideas of rationality and obligation, we might follow the Buddhist approach. From the beginning, Gautama the Buddha, the founder of Buddhism, made it clear that the goal of his teaching was to eliminate suffering. Actions that contribute to the elimination of suffering in ourselves and others are considered recommendable in Buddhist teachings. Conversely, actions that cause suffering to ourselves and others are considered unrecommendable. The former are known as *kusala*, or wholesome actions, and the latter as *akusala*, or unwholesome actions. This distinction serves as the foundation of Buddhist ethics.

Suffering arises from various sources. Three "poisons"—greed, anger, and ignorance—are considered the primary causes of suffering in early Buddhism. This diagnosis provides a comprehensive understanding of human actions and interactions, encompassing intention, desire, emotions, and mental capacity. Greed is the desire to possess various objects. Anger, though not as intentional, is also fueled by negative emotions. Ignorance, perhaps the least intentional, is regarded as the root cause of suffering in Buddhism.

What causes suffering must be violent in its appearance. Suffering arises because of the violence in an action, and violence is not monolithic. The logic of exclusion that I explored in this chapter is based primarily on violence and leads to violence, which in turn causes suffering in those subjected to the exclusion. This prompts me to examine the nature and scope of violence, which is the topic of the next chapter.

3

Violence

On the day the woman heard the story of Gwangju for the first time, she went to Incheon, a port city about sixteen miles northwest of Seoul. This wasn't her intended destination; it was simply the farthest place she could go to by subway. Nowadays many people, especially non-Koreans, recognize this city because of Incheon International Airport, but that didn't exist at the time of her visit. In those days, Peace Park was one of the main attractions of the city, both for tourists and locals. When the woman arrived in Incheon, she couldn't think of any specific place to go, so she wandered to Peace Park, where pigeons, the symbols of peace in Korea as in many other cultures, were leisurely pecking at grains strewn by tourists. The world must be at peace, she thought, even though that was the opposite of how she felt that day.

S. Y., who had told the woman about Gwangju, was a high school student when the uprising took place in the city. "We all went out to the street to join the protest," he had said.

"High school students joined that bloody protest?" the woman asked.

"Yes, we did," S. Y. replied. Students from Jeonnam National University had marched in the protest demanding democracy, and the military interim government had mobilized paratroopers to suppress the demonstrators. The people of Gwangju joined the demonstration, and it soon turned into a conflict between the people of Gwangju and the government of the Republic of Korea.

The woman's sister, who was living in the United States, called their mother around the time of the Gwangju uprising to ask whether they were safe. "We are all doing well," her mother said. "Everything is okay here in Seoul." What the woman's sister saw through news media outside of South Korea was not available in Seoul, where the media was completely controlled by the government. Some forty years later, the movie *A Taxi Driver* (2017) told the story of German journalist Jürgen Hinzpeter (1937–2016), who witnessed and photographed the massacre in Gwangju and managed to smuggle out his film rolls wrapped as cookies.

Since the day I went to Incheon over four decades ago, I have often wondered what I had in mind at Peace Park that day. What was I doing there, feeding grains to the pigeons, my mind still in shock with visions of bloody protesters? I needed to process what I had just heard from S. Y.—that the government had used military force to kill its own people who were protesting in demand of democracy. Student demonstrations were a part of college life in South Korea in the 1970s and early 1980s. The smell of tear gas was a fixture on college campuses in those days, but the degree of violence and the brutality with which the protests in Gwangju were controlled was different. I felt lost.

Years later, after the Tiananmen Square massacre in China in 1989, I could not help but remember Gwangju. A well-known image shows a Chinese man with a plastic bag in his hand standing in front of a line of tanks, as if he could stop the entire army with his fragile body. What was he thinking? Like the girl covered in napalm running away naked during the Vietnam War, as if running could help her escape from the pain of her burned body, he looks strikingly weak in the presence of the power and violence confronting him. He stands in front of the tanks like the last conscience of the people against state violence, the hope that one can still stand against that violence even in the face of power displayed at such magnitude. The napalm girl, whose image was captured in the Pulitzer Prize–winning photograph "The Terror of War," has since grown up and now lives in the United States. No information is available about what happened to the tank man after the incident.

Years later still, I discussed the Tiananmen Square incident, also known as the June Fourth Massacre, while teaching my class on modern East Asia. Afterward, a Chinese student came up to me and said that she had never heard of the incident. Does history repeat itself?

What is violence? How do we define it? Why do we use violence? And who justifies it? Is violence justifiable in any situation?

A former colleague of mine, Jeffrey Reiman, and his coauthor Paul Leighton, invited their readers to take part in a thought experiment in his book on criminal justice in the United States, *The Rich Get Richer and the Poor Get Prison*:

> Think of a crime, any crime. Picture the first crime that comes into your mind. What do you see? The odds are you are not imagining a meatpacking executive sitting at his desk, calculating the costs of proper safety precautions and deciding not to invest in them. Probably what you do see with your mind's eye is one person assaulting another physically and robbing something from another via the threat of physical attack. Look more closely. What does the attacker look like? It's a safe bet he (and it is a *he*, of course) is not wearing a suit and tie. In fact, you—like us, like almost anyone else in America—picture a young, tough, lower-class male when the thought of crime first pops into your head.[1]

In this book, Reiman and Leighton demonstrate with ample data how white-collar criminals often evade the legal system while people living under the poverty line and in underprivileged environments are easily caught and punished by the US criminal justice system. Exploring the "relationship between economic status and arrest, conviction, and sentencing,"[2] they argue that *"the criminal justice system fails in the fight against crime while making it look as if crime is the work of the poor."*[3]

The above thought experiment reveals how naive people can be about their perceptions of crime, and this naiveté contributes to the perpetuation of injustice against the poor. In the introduction to the thirteenth edition of this book, published in 2023, which provides extensive records of promises for criminal justice reform made by presidents and political parties in the forty years since the first edition in 1979, Reiman and Leighton note, "We are still confronted with the specter of a large and scary population of poor criminals. And the criminal justice system still fails to protect us from the well-off by *not* treating their harmful acts as crimes."[4] Replace "crime" in the above passages with "violence." Most of us can understand violence in a manner similar to Reiman and Leighton's thought experiment on crime. Upon reflection, we come to realize that the source of violence in our society runs much deeper than the superficial display of what we typically consider violence.

In *Of Grammatology*, Derrida defined three layers of violence. He argued that violence begins with language. Linguistic violence is not limited to curses and slurs; rather, the logic of curses and slurs aligns with the logic of linguistic violence. When someone hears a curse or a slur, it prompts an inflammatory reaction because it does not align with how they would identify themselves. The power of a curse comes from its defamatory effect, as the person against whom it is used refuses to be characterized by it. A curse or a slur does not allow for ambiguity, unlike other linguistic expressions; it means what it means. A curse maximizes its effect through its reductionist nature.

To a different degree, though, language functions primarily to define things and give them names. The Swiss linguist Ferdinand de Saussure (1857–1913) argued that linguistic signs are based on an arbitrary system. For example, the word "apple"—that is, *a, p, p, l, e* in English—has nothing to do with the round red, green, or yellow fruit. On the basis of a socially agreed convention, we use the expression to refer to the fruit. With the example of an

63

apple, this arbitrary system does not seem to create much of a problem. As language users, we have simply agreed on an arbitrary connection between a name and a referent.

The situation is not as simple with expressions like "white," "a woman," or "an Asian." There might be a difference in degree, but linguistic expressions constantly and systematically shape the user's understanding of a thing or a being. Defying the boundaries set by linguistic conventions and practices requires challenging the entire structure of social organization and value system. When someone is identified as an "Asian woman," the connotation is clear: the person is not white, in the white-centered world, and she is not a man, in a patriarchal society. The expression "an Asian woman" quickly places the person on the margin of the margin. Her position is already situated within the grand structure of the world in which the white male takes center stage. Her qualifications, preferences, and life story are often understood within this context. Derrida defines this practice of language as linguistic violence.

The second layer of violence relates to laws, morality, and ethical values in society. How can laws be violence? Aren't they created to protect people from violence? Laws and constitutions are created to preserve human dignity and protect people from violence, but they are also made by human beings, which means by those who hold the power in society to make them—typically those representing the voice of the center. We might want to believe that those who participated in legislation could not intentionally create rules that discriminate against those who are not in a position to participate in the legislative process. But history proves that the situation is not that simple.

The landmark US Supreme Court case *Brown v. Board of Education* (1954) ruled that segregation in public schools violates the US Constitution. This ruling marked an important step for racial justice in American society. But it also revealed how biased and discriminatory the legal process could be, and had been, by showing that what American society had upheld as constitutional for over half a century was, in fact, a biased practice.

The 1896 case *Plessy v. Ferguson* ruled that segregated education in public schools does not violate the Fourteenth Amendment of the US Constitution, which asserts that no state in the United States shall "deny to any person within its jurisdiction the equal protection of the laws." Better known for its claim of "separate but equal," this court ruling justified discrimination in American society as constitutional for more than half a century. Throughout the famed trial of *Brown v. Board of Education*, Thurgood Marshall's team struggled to prove that segregation in public schools was unconstitutional.

We might think this case would be an exception, but a Supreme Court case and ruling does not emerge from an isolated incident. Rather, the case crystallized a problem in American society that was backed by the legality of the US Constitution, which violated the constitutional rights of people of color. What else can we call this but legal violence? The power and danger of legal violence, like linguistic violence, lies in its collectivity. When we say "linguistic violence" or "legal violence" we do not mean that an individual struck another person, even though both might impose the social structure that would lead an individual to behave in that manner. Instead, both linguistic and legal violence are structural forms of violence that require addressing the structure of our society and engaging in collective efforts to identify and mitigate this violence.

Derrida characterized a third level of violence encompassing more visible forms of violence such as rape, war, state violence, and police brutality. Franz Fanon, who offered a nuanced discussion of the use of violence in colonial and postcolonial contexts, used the expression "atmosphere of violence" to describe how violence permeates our lifeworld. Violence is structural; it constitutes the atmosphere of social and political life. Like atmosphere, which does not clearly divide the public world from the personal, or the social-political world from an individual's daily life, the atmosphere of violence filters through various dimensions and venues of our existence in innumerably different forms.

The contemporary Korean writer Han Kang, who received the Nobel Prize in Literature in 2024, reveals the pervasiveness of violence—or the atmosphere of violence, to use Fanon's expression—from the perspective of an individual's daily life in *The Vegetarian* (2007). In the story, a housewife named Yeong-hye, whom her husband describes as "completely unremarkable in every way,"[5] suddenly refuses one day to eat meat. Her family, including her husband, finds her action absurd at best and tries to persuade her to stop what they see as nonsensical. From this brief summary of the main plot, one might assume the story centers on the ethics of a vegetarian diet. While the spirit of vegetarianism, which opposes violence against animals, indeed relates to the narrative, the violence portrayed in the story has a far more complex structure.

What triggered the sudden change in Yeong-hye's life is a dream in which she finds herself chewing on raw red meat, her clothes soaked with blood, in a place where people seem to be enjoying a barbecue party. Fear overwhelms her as she sees herself in the mirror, which reflects a total stranger. The day after having the dream, she throws out all the meats in her fridge: beef for shabu-shabu, pork belly, beef shin, squid, sliced eel, dried croaker fish, and so on.

Her husband believes she has lost her mind, and her family members view her behavior as irrational. Her father even tries to force-feed her meat. Meanwhile, her dreams continue, revealing the nature of the violence inscribed in her memory. Through these dreams, readers learn that she was bitten by a dog as a child. Upset by the incident, her father had the dog tied to a motorcycle, which he rode around the village. On the seventh round, the dog—exhausted from trying to keep up with the motorcycle—was dragged and eventually died, bleeding from its mouth. The villagers had a party that day with dog soup, which Yeong-hye savored. "Is this a story of trauma?" we might ask. But the ending of the novel offers a different perspective on violence. In the final scene, Yeong-hye sits on a hospital bench, naked from the waist up, holding something in her hand. In her fist, her husband finds a small, white-eyed bird, crunched to death.

Different types of violence overlap in this story, both implicitly and explicitly. Yeong-hye's obscure but determined awareness of the problem of meat-eating relates unambiguously to the violence of humans against other beings. Her family members' violence against her for her

67

determination to not eat meat reveals the violence in human relationships dominated by power dynamics. When she refuses her father's order to eat meat, he slaps her. Neither her husband nor her family members even try to understand why Yeong-hye has suddenly changed; from their perspective, she is wrong, irrational, and even out of her mind.

Normalcy, both mental and physical, is defined by those who consider themselves to hold the central power in the relationship—in this case, Yeong-hye's father, as the head of the family; her husband, in the patriarchal relationship between husband and wife; and other family members, considered a group of right-minded people within this con-struction of normalcy—and condemns the margin without examining the nature of Yeong-hye's actions. In this con-text, violence against Yeong-hye becomes violence done to women; the author repeatedly emphasizes Yeong-hye's nakedness and reveals her breasts as a symbol of nonvio-lence. But Yeong-hye is not an innocent victim of violence. In her dreams, she did not withdraw from the violence done to the dog; rather, she relished the dog soup after the dog was killed. At the end of the story, Yeong-hye is the one who inflicts violence on the bird, despite her opposition to meat-eating and her resistance to conforming to violence.

In the second story of this tripartite novel, Yeong-hye confesses that it was not in fact just the meat-eating that she found repulsive: "I thought it was all because of eating meat. . . . I thought all I had to do was to stop eating meat and then the faces wouldn't come back. But it didn't work." Yeong-hye realizes the source of violence lies deeper than meat-eating, saying, "Now I know. The face is inside my stomach. It rose up from inside my stomach."[6] The capacity for violence has a deeper origin, as does the trauma caused by it. In the story, the author does not explicitly identify the deep source of violence and trauma, but we can trace it further, even though we cannot definitively pinpoint its origin.

Han Kang was born in 1970 in Gwangju, a city in the southern part of South Korea. In contemporary Korean history, Gwangju signifies more than just a city; it represents the Gwangju Uprising, also known as the Gwangju Democratization Movement, which took place in the spring of 1980, as I briefly described at the beginning of this chapter.

In South Korea, the academic year begins on March 2. In March 1980, with the start of the new semester, professors and students expelled for prodemocracy activities returned to their universities and formed student unions. These unions led nationwide demonstrations for reforms, including an end to the martial law that had been declared after the assassination of then-president Park Chung-Hee (1917–1979), who had ruled South Korea for almost two decades. Student protests demanding democracy, workers' rights, minimum wages, and freedom of the press had been significant features of South Korea in the 1970s.

On May 18, 1980, students gathered at the gate of Jeonnam National University to protest its closure, which was intended to preempt student demonstrations. While student protests were common in South Korea at the time, the government reacted differently toward them than it had in other cases. This time, it mobilized paratroopers and engaged in acts of severe brutality against the students in Gwangju. "The students were beaten, clubbed, knifed and bayonetted,"[7] assert Gi-Wook Shin and Kyung Moon

Hwang in *Contentious Kwangju: The May 18 Uprising in Korea's Past and Present.*[8]

The next day, having witnessed the brutality with which students were treated, citizens joined the student protesters. Martial law soldiers again attacked the protesting crowds. On May 20, some 30,000 to 40,000 citizens joined the protest, and soldiers opened fire on the demonstrators. A war between the Korean Army and the citizens of Gwangju began.[9] In reaction, the people of Gwangju began to arm themselves, creating the Citizens' Army, and captured the Provincial Office (May 21–26), demanding the government engage in negotiations with them. For several days after the Citizens' Army occupied the provincial building, the protesters seemed to be winning, and negotiations with the government seemed imminent. But on May 27, the government mobilized the military and attacked the Citizens' Army and the people of Gwangju, bringing the resistance to an end.[10]

By the end of the ten days spanning from May 18 to May 27, 1980, an estimated "five hundred civilians [were] dead and over three thousand injured,"[11] write Shin and Hwang. Communication and media were strictly controlled, so people outside of the city remained unaware of what was happening in Gwangju. Not until the 1990s were the victims officially memorialized, and novels, TV dramas, and movies began to depict the incident, although some literary works started addressing it in the late 1980s.[12]

State violence is the ultimate form of the center's mutilation of the margin in the modern nation-state. The nation-state is the only institution in modern times with the legal authority to use violence. This privilege was granted to the state so it could protect its people, but the nation-state has used its power to suppress its people as much as to protect them. The legality or constitutionality of an action does not necessarily mean that it is justifiable or free from violence. No social laws are natural; they are created by humans, which means they are products of the center. As much as laws are supposed to protect people, their origins—that is, rationales created by the privileged—and the reality of their execution that reinforces the privilege of the executor generate violence against those who are excluded from the creation and enforcement of the laws.

Walter Benjamin (1892–1940), a German thinker who committed suicide to avoid being repatriated to the Nazis, must have given considerable thought to the violence of the state. In his renowned 1921 essay "Towards the Critique of Violence," Benjamin refers to the violence that gives rise to the law as "law-making violence" and to the violence of the state in enforcing the law as "law-preserving violence."

In his discussion of violence, Benjamin introduces another type, which he calls "divine violence." He contrasts divine violence with law-making and law-preserving violence, characterizing it as "law-destroying." While law-making and law-preserving violence establish boundaries, divine violence, according to Benjamin, "boundlessly destroys them." He further explains that while law-making violence "brings at once guilt and retribution," divine violence only "expiates."[13] To Benjamin, divine violence is violence in the sense that it destroys that which destroys. But it does so without creating divisions between inside and outside, generating a sense of guilt, or following a desire for vengeance—common elements that accompany legal procedure.

Whether the use of the word "violence" in the expression "divine violence" is appropriate remains a subject of debate. In this concept, Benjamin was envisioning liberation from violence through the force that would dismantle the violence that afflicts people within a nation-state, along with the inevitable entanglement in social structures such as law-making and law-preserving functions that results. Liberation is not meant to occur exclusively for a specific group; nor should it create another boundary in the name of liberation. Since the boundaries that give rise to violence need to be dismantled, liberation through divine violence must bring liberation for all. In this sense, such liberation should be "divine"—something that transcends the human propensity for creating boundaries and separating the self from others.

Han Kang and her family left Gwangju several months before the Gwangju Uprising. Survivor's guilt and an exploration of violence would become central themes in her works. In *Human Acts* (2014), a novel published seven years after *The Vegetarian*, Han directly addresses the Gwangju Uprising. Spanning the period from the Gwangju Uprising in May 1980 to 2010, *Human Acts* tells the stories of six people whose lives were brutally affected by the incident. Two of the narrators are killed during the uprising, while the other four survive, grappling with trauma, memories, and mourning. The original Korean title of the novel, *Sonyŏn i onda* (A boy is coming), refers to a boy named Dong-ho, a ninth-grader killed in the final stage of the uprising, whose story the novel begins with.

Han Kang employs the device of having a dead person as a narrator, telling his story from the world of the dead, which intensifies the effect of the massacre's horrific reality. Dong-ho narrates that he came to the Provincial Office, where the Citizens' Army was stationed, in search of his friend Jeong-dae, who had gone missing amid the chaos of the conflict. In the Provincial Office, the boy sees dead bodies lined up in various rooms. Once family members identify a body, the corpse is placed in a coffin covered with the national flag of South Korea, and a simplified form of a funeral ritual is performed, during which the national anthem of South Korea is sung. Dong-ho asks, "Why would you sing the national anthem for people who'd been killed by soldiers? Why cover the coffin with the national flag? As though it wasn't the nation itself that had murdered them."[14]

The boy's poignant question reveals the irony in state violence and the murky reality in which people are trapped within a nation-state. Being a member of a nation-state in the modern world is not an optional element of human existence. Lacking citizenship means being a stateless person, without protection; moreover, that person's life activities would be drastically limited, as the nation-state serves as the basic unit through which the world functions in our time. When a country utilizes its capacity for violence against its own people instead of protecting them, those who become the targets of such violence not only lack the means to protect themselves but also face the ironic situation articulated by Dong-ho, the middle-schooler in this story. Should people disown the state because state violence is killing its citizens? If so, where would they go? Who would protect them? Should people still regard the nation as their own country when the nation uses violence against them? In the international community, procedures for refugees and asylum seekers were introduced to assist people in such situations. But refugee status is granted only in extreme cases of political insecurity, war, or religious persecution. Meanwhile, the majority of those who have been or are subjected to state violence or discrimination remain helpless in the face of the nation-state's brutality.

Marginalized groups are the most vulnerable to such maneuvers, as they often have limited or no resources with which to challenge structurally constructed violence and discrimination. Are the state that killed the protesters and the state whose anthem and flag were solemnized at the protesters' funerals two different entities? Obedience to, worship of, and respect for one's nation are still expected, even when the nation-state discriminates and uses violence against its people. After Dong-ho's death, his brother pledges revenge for his sibling. But their mother asks her son, "How would it be possible to take revenge for your brother when it was the country that killed him?"[15] Indeed, who should be the target of revenge for state violence, if such revenge were to be planned?

In 2016, the American football quarterback Colin Kaepernick of the San Francisco 49ers sparked controversy by kneeling during the playing of the American national anthem before a game. Through his peaceful protest, he aimed to raise awareness about police brutality and racism against Black Americans. Responses to the incident were divided: some praised him for his social awareness, while others criticized him for being disrespectful and unpatriotic.

Rituals act as a condensed form of the social bond and uphold society's demand for conformity among its members. The heavy symbolism of the national anthem and flag burdens individuals and traps them, even when these symbols represent the society's structural violence. Furthermore, symbols of the nation-state are not limited to ritualized items like the national anthem or flag; they also function in language, with one representative example being the word "patriotism." The word "patriot" originates from the Greek expression *patēr*, meaning "father"; thus, a patriot is someone related to the father. It has come to mean "fellow countrymen" and signify love of one's country. Like most forms of love, such as romantic love or love for an object, love of one's country can easily go awry. Whereas obedience can quickly be recognized as problematic in a romantic relationship or between friends, the love of country demands unchallenged submission and the demonstration of an individual's or group's contributions and subordination to that nation-state. What if a member of society believes that the country is doing something wrong? How much space does that member have to challenge the country without being criticized as unpatriotic?

During the Pacific War, Japanese Sōtō Zen–trained suicide pilots, known as kamikaze (literally meaning "god's wind"), were deployed to attack the Allies in an effort to demonstrate Buddhism's usefulness to the Japanese Empire, even though such involvement contradicted the fundamental Buddhist principle of not harming living beings. Some might adopt a sympathetic view toward Japanese Buddhism's involvement with the Japanese war effort, seeing it as a desperate attempt by the marginalized to survive. Following the Meiji Restoration in 1868, Japan suppressed Buddhism as a "foreign" religion, promoting Shinto, the indigenous Japanese faith, to solidify national identity. In this context of marginalization, certain branches of Japanese Buddhism, such as the Sōtō Zen school, aligned with Japan's military efforts to demonstrate Buddhism's contribution to the Japanese Empire. War, unlike everyday events, complicates any challenge to the center.

A Japanese exchange student in my class once gave a presentation on kamikaze and Japanese Sōtō Zen's involvement in the war, framing it as the Buddhist way of showing compassion. The student argued that the goal of Buddhist teaching is to eliminate suffering, and that both Sōtō Zen practitioners and the kamikaze sacrificed themselves to save the Japanese people from suffering. I countered by pointing out that they did so by causing suffering to others. The student refused to accept my argument, asserting that Japanese soldiers and Japanese Buddhism had a responsibility to the Japanese people, not to their enemies.

During the Pacific War, an estimated 80,000 to 200,000 women were subjected to sex slavery to satisfy Japanese soldiers' sexual desires, with an estimated 80 percent of these women being Korean. Sexual slavery is itself a grave issue that warrants careful exploration, but the situations endured by former "comfort women" present a more complex picture wherein gender, culture, and nationalism become interwoven. The practice of sex slavery through the comfort stations occurred from the late 1930s until the 1940s, but it was not until the 1990s that the stories of these women began to gain widespread attention. A former comfort woman, Kim Hak Soon (1924–1997), became the first to offer a public testimony about the issue. In 1998, the UN Human Rights Commission launched an investigation into the matter and passed a resolution declaring that a violation of women's rights is a violation of human rights. The issue of comfort women is, on the surface, an epitome of the commodification of women and their bodies. Commodification here does not refer to selling for profit, but rather to the reduction of women's existence to their bodies, which are further degraded as tradable and disposable objects devoid of life, meaning, and dignity.

The predicament of women in a patriarchal system is not limited to the commodification of their lives and bodies. We must ask why it took so long for the former comfort women to acknowledge the obvious fact that they were victims of sex slavery. Almost half a century passed before Kim Hak Soon gathered the courage to reveal her identity as a former comfort woman and testify to the inhumane conditions she had to endure at "comfort stations." The cruelty did not end with the destruction of the comfort stations and the conclusion of the war. When the former comfort women returned home, they were unable to reveal what had happened to them, as their societies would not accept women whose bodies had been "spoiled." The physical violence enacted upon women's bodies at the comfort stations continued in the form of cultural and social violence, which upheld the purity of women's bodies as a norm in their patriarchal society.

Social violence normalizes harm and provides justification for the harm done, bringing about a second form of violence. The societies of the former comfort women refused to properly acknowledge the violence to which these women had been subjected, shaming the victims by emphasizing the importance of chastity and purity for women's bodies. This secondary violence added further injury to women who had already been severely abused.

The issue of comfort women is fundamentally a women's issue, but nationalism became a significant barrier to the evolution of the investigation and the demand for justice for the former comfort women. Rather than being just one element among the diverse factors that allowed the exploitation of these women to occur, nationalism was one of its main causes. What happens, then, when feminism, which challenges the millennia-old ideology of patriarchy, encounters nationalism?

In her discussion of comfort women, the Japanese sociologist Ueno Chizuko asks: Can feminism transcend nationalism? Ueno's question serves as a poignant warning that hierarchy dominates not only human relationships and social structures but also the world of ideology. As Ueno unambiguously expresses, "Feminism was the demon child that was paradoxically born out of the innate contradiction of the modern period."[16] The official promise of modernity demands freedom and equality for all. Feminism and women's movements emerged from the pursuit of these promises, embodying the very ideals of modern times. The reality of modernity, however, is that only certain groups of people are free and equal, while others are relegated to the status of second-class citizens.

The idea of the equality of all beings in the modernist project did not include women, people of color, factory workers, or the have-nots. Hence, as Ueno tells us, "female citizenship" is a "logical paradox."[17] A nation-state promises equality and freedom for its citizens, yet women remain in a subjugated position in patriarchal society, which the nation-states continue to uphold. This paradox enables situations like the sex slavery of women through comfort stations. In investigating the situation, the nation-state once again takes a privileged position; as a result, the issue of comfort women was understood more as part of the conflict between South Korea and Japan rather than as a profound case of the subjugation of women by male ideology that has occurred throughout patriarchal history.

Ueno, however, does not support the naive idea that women are simply innocent victims of the violence of the nation-state. As discussed earlier, Han Kang questioned the possibility of completely staying away from violence through the character of Yeong-hye, who suffered from patriarchal and social violence but also realized her own participation in imposing violence on others. Ueno reveals that in order for Japanese women to gain recognition as members of the nation-state, they needed to be present at the crime scene. Japanese women, Ueno argues, are not immune to the violence of Japanese imperialism in their treatment of other women. The eugenic project supported by Japanese New Women during the height of the Pacific War demonstrates that women in a nation-state are not just victims but can also victimize other women for the benefit of the nation-state as they try to prove their value within it. During the height of the Pacific War, a eugenics policy was implemented to increase population, including "who was qualified for motherhood and who was not?"[18] Hiratsuka Raichō, a leading feminist at the time, welcomed this national control of women's reproduction in the name of "protection of the family system." In this framework, women were meant to be wives and mothers, while men were expected to be strong to fight for the imperialist goals. But as Ueno writes, "In its shadow were the military comfort women who were forced to carry the burden of 'whorishness' as opposed to motherhood, the dark side of the sexual double standard."[19]

The former comfort women remained silenced for half a century; to varying degrees, women have been silenced for millennia, as symbolically portrayed in the case of Yeong-hye in *The Vegetarian*. When women try to tell their stories, their words often fail to receive the attention they deserve. Even worse, the reliability and authenticity of women's words are frequently called into question. Yeong-hye's family dismissed her behavior as nonsensical when she declared that she would not eat meat, and the testimonies of the former comfort women repeatedly met with criticisms that delegitimized their claims.

The feminist philosopher Miranda Fricker's concept of "epistemic injustice" can aid in explaining this phenomenon. Fricker uses this term to denote the refusal to accept the validity of knowledge based on the knower's position. When a piece of information or an idea is expressed, the validity of the information is judged not only by its content but also by the knower's position in society, which causes unfair and discriminatory understanding of the provided knowledge. Fricker identifies two forms of epistemic injustice: testimonial injustice and hermeneutical injustice. When the former comfort women sought to tell their stories, they found their credibility constantly put on trial. Some people claimed they were paid and therefore were prostitutes, not sex slaves. Others argued that sex stations have existed throughout history whenever and wherever there were wars or military bases. Still others maintained that the Japanese government had no involvement in the management of the comfort stations.

Research shows that most of the former comfort women came from rural areas or financially destitute families.

Most of them belonged to socially marginalized groups, making them triply or quadruply marginalized: citizens of colonized countries, women in a patriarchal culture, people from rural areas in a modern urban-centered world, and individuals from financially underprivileged backgrounds in a capitalist society. The credibility of their testimonies was constantly undermined by their quadruple-minority positions. Fricker calls this phenomenon a "credibility deficit," in which the speaker receives "less credibility than she otherwise would have" for her testimony because of her social position, leading to prejudicial dysfunction.[20] The opposite case involves a "credibility excess," in which the knower receives more credibility than they deserve because of their social position.

Injustice is embedded in our language, modes of thinking, and social structures, exerting its power even before any actions are taken by an individual, as I discussed through the concepts of "preemptive exclusion" or "unexamined exclusion" in chapter 2. A foundational logic of violence is reductionism. When a being is reduced to a single expression (such as a slur), or to skin color, gender, or ethnicity, the multidimensionality of existence—what we call life—fails to manifest its creativity, becoming stifled and further weakening the capacity of those at the margins. The vicious cycle then continues.

Patriarchy is as oppressive as nationalism because both function through reductionism. As Ueno states, "Just as I cannot be reduced to the category 'woman,' do not reduce me to the category 'national subject.'"[21] Ueno does not completely deny the functionality of these categories; rather, she urges us to "relativize these categories." Reductionism forecloses the full range of possibilities of a being.

When I am identified as an Asian woman, I am reduced to two categories whose meanings have already been largely predetermined. Once an individual's life becomes reduced to these predefined categories by society, in order to transcend those stereotypes, they must invest extra time and effort just to show others that their existence is far more complex and richer than the categories to which they have been reduced. As the Nobel Prize–winning writer Toni Morrison once said,

> The function, the very serious function of racism is distraction. It keeps you from doing your work. It keeps you explaining over and over again your reason for being. Somebody says you have no language and you spend twenty years proving that you do. Somebody says your head isn't shaped properly so you have scientists working on the fact that it is. Somebody says you have no art, so you dredge that up. Somebody says you have no kingdoms, so you dredge those up. None of this is necessary. There will always be one more thing.[22]

For a person at the margin, existence is defined by their marginal position, not by their personality, characters, or merit.

Against the constant reductionism of the self that leads to violence, we can consider the Buddhist idea of the self as an alternative. As we briefly touched upon in previous chapters, the Buddhist worldview proposes that things in the world exist through causes and conditions, not through any enduring essence of a being. Because a being does not possess a permanent independent essence, the Buddhist self is called "no-self." No-self does not mean that one does not exist; rather, one exists without a reducible, permanent essence, hence no-(permanent)-self.

But what does it mean, exactly, to say that a person does not have a permanent and independent self? How does the Buddhist proposal explain the undeniable fact that I am not you or them? What would Buddhism say about the simple fact that I am different from other people—that I have my own past, thoughts, family, education, cultural background, and so on? Simply put, I have my own life that distinguishes me from others.

The Buddhist proposal of the no-self has been maintained for more than two millennia across various Buddhist schools, but this does not make the concept easier to understand. The Buddhist no-self can sound counterintuitive or nonsensical. But it sounds like nonsense only when we approach this proposal through the lens of our familiar individualistic views of the self. In modern times, the individual's autonomy and rights have been central to defining the value of a person. This individualistic perspective, which places emphasis on a permanent, independent self, stands in stark contrast with the Buddhist view, which sees the self as fluid and interdependent, shaped by the ever-changing conditions of life.

We must put this approach in perspective, however. The emphasis on individual autonomy and rights has been necessary to challenge and correct premodern societies in which a monarch or a transcendental being controlled the individual's existence. To legitimize human dignity and capacities without anchoring them to a higher being, highlighting the individual's autonomy and rights was essential. More than two hundred years after the introduction of these claims, the pendulum has swung to the opposite extreme. For some groups of people, autonomy and rights still remain beyond reach, atop mountains they struggle to climb. For others, claims to autonomy and rights are understood without the accompanying responsibilities, resulting in a constant expansion of the meaning of the "I."

The understanding of the self as an independent individual closely relates to the use of violence, as Judith Butler eloquently explains in *The Force of Nonviolence*. When a person inflicts harm on other beings, the assumption must be that the harm will not have a substantial effect on the life of the harmer. The self who does violence and the beings on whom the violence is inflicted must be seen as distinctly separate for the logic of violence to function. The Buddhist no-self theory proposes a scenario different from such a dualistic vision of the self. If an individual's existence is connected to that of others through various causes and conditions, they cannot completely shield themselves from the violence they impose on others. If individuals believed that violence inflicted on others would also harm themselves, they would hesitate before resorting to violence. In this view, the self and others are not distinctly separate beings; rather, their interdependence means that harm inflicted on others inevitably affects them as well.

The logic of individualism, when viewed in the context of violence, aligns with my discussion of reductionism. I cannot be reduced to just a woman or a citizen of a nation-state, and similarly, I cannot be reduced to just an individual with a fixed identity or self. An individual's existence should be richer and broader than such a limited identity allows. The Buddhist no-self can thus be understood as an openness of the self, rather than as the nonexistence of the self. In the context of no-self, I am who I am, and the

Buddhist no-self aligns with Derrida's vision of "the irre-
ducibility of *who* to *what*,"[23] where "what" is understood as
a fixed essence.

Violence occurs when this irreducible reality of existence
is trampled, and "what" demands "who" to be "what." The
"I," understood as the no-self, refuses to be reduced to any
specific category, such as gender, nationality, social class, or
sexual orientation. The "I," as the no-self, must accept that it
embodies all the relevant categories and more, and that
these categories are creatively interwoven into an individual's life—not only for them but with others, who also exist
through the intertwined web of categories and meaning-
producing mechanisms in the sociopolitical milieu. This is
why, on the flip side, considering intersectionality proves
essential to gauging the meaning and value of a being or an
incident. No being is an island, and individuality should not
be understood as meaning a person has a single identifiable
element to define them, but rather, that each being exists in
an intricate web of different elements that constantly create
meanings about the being.

The more reductionist a group's sense of identity, the
more devastating its effect on those at the margin becomes.
Each society has mechanisms to place certain groups at
the margin and keep them there. Some of these mechanisms are centuries old, while others emerge in response
to the changing dynamics of society. In the next chapter I
examine some of the apparatuses through which the center keeps the margin at the margin.

4

Minority Against Minority

L os Angeles was burning. Olympic Boulevard, where Korean-owned stores were congregated, was consumed by glaring flames on the TV screen in the woman's small living room. As the blaze continued late into the night, her eyes remained fixed on the flames flickering on the screen. All four white police officers indicted for beating an African American man named Rodney King had been acquitted, sparking a protest that escalated into riots, with stores mostly owned by Korean Americans being set on fire.

"How does the logic work here?" the woman asked herself, watching the flames on the TV screen. White police officers had been acquitted of the charge of beating an African American man, which enraged the African American community, so they burned stores owned by Korean Americans? Things didn't add up. The woman wondered why the African Americans' rage against white people was directed not toward them, but instead, toward Korean Americans. And could it be only African Americans who found the verdict unjust? What about white Americans? Did they all agree with the verdict? That couldn't be. To answer these questions, the woman realized she had to delve into the migration histories of Korean Americans, Asian Americans, and African Americans, as well as the history of US immigration policy and racism in America. A journey had begun for her.

This all happened only a few years after I came to the United States. I had yet to familiarize myself with the depth of racism and the complex relationships among different ethnic groups in America. I was only slowly learning that, in the United States, I was not just a woman—the identity I had struggled to overcome in South Korea. Now, I was an Asian woman: a double minority. The night I watched LA burning on my TV was one of the defining moments that forced me to confront the reality of ethnic conflicts and racism in America.

The incident, known as the 1992 Los Angeles riots, occurred in late April and early May of that year. That summer, I traveled to Los Angeles—my first trip to the West Coast—and went to Olympic Boulevard directly from the LA airport. I wanted to see the place that had been on fire a couple of months earlier. Many stores were still closed, the stains of the fires still visible. In those soot-covered ruins must have been buried the stories of so many immigrants—their work, struggles, dreams, and despair.

Thirty years later, an old friend of mine asked me to do him a favor and give an interview for his daughter's doctoral project on the relationship between Korean Americans and African Americans, and I couldn't say no. The sociology doctoral candidate asked me interview questions such as, "What is your impression of African Americans?"

and "What do you think about their relationship to Korean Americans?"

Why focus on the relationship between Korean Americans and African Americans in American society, rather than that between Korean Americans and Anglo-Americans, I wondered? Wouldn't the latter make more sense, given the power structure in American society? Or shouldn't the question of the relationship between Korean and African Americans be explored alongside an investigation of the role of white America in shaping this relationship? But I did not raise these questions with the doctoral candidate.

The history of Korean immigration to the United States began in 1903, when 103 Koreans landed in Hawai'i as laborers for the sugar cane fields. From 1903 to 1905, an estimated seven thousand Koreans migrated to the United States, with some later moving to the mainland. But it was not until the 1960s, which brought the reform of immigration laws, that a significant number of Koreans began migrating to the United States.

With the civil rights movement of the early 1960s, the US immigration policy based on the National Origins Formula came under attack as racial discrimination, as it limited immigration by non-Northern Europeans and operated through a quota system based on national origin, race, creed, and color. In response to this criticism, a new policy was introduced. The 1965 Immigration Act, originally known as the Immigration and Nationality Act of 1965, prioritized family reunification as well as immigration by professionals and skilled workers. This new immigration policy would permanently alter the demographics of immigration populations in the United States.

With the 1965 Immigration Act, Korean professionals were welcomed into the United States. The US government had calculated that bringing scientists, doctors, and other professionals to the country would strengthen its economy. Criticized as a "brain drain" for Korea, this immigration policy raised ethical questions about the international flow of people and migration, as it rendered poor countries even poorer through the emigration of their "brains" to wealthier countries like the United States.

By the late 1970s, the number of Korean professionals moving to the United States had declined, but the 1965 Immigration Act changed US demographics more significantly than policymakers had anticipated. Koreans who were already living in the United States invited their family members, and just as many nonprofessional workers as professionals began arriving. Koreatown began taking shape in Los Angeles. According to the author of *Koreatown, Los Angeles* (2022), a popular origin story of Koreatown marks its beginning in October 1971, when Hi Duk Lee, a South Korean immigrant who came to the United States via Germany, opened his Olympic Market on West Olympic Boulevard. Olympic Market, according to Lee, was the "first true Korean grocery store that was not a wholesaler."[1]

Lee arrived in LA in 1967 and had managed to open a market in just four years. In the six years following the opening of his store, "he grew his business twentyfold."[2] That was indeed a Korean immigrant's success story. By the late 1970s, Koreatown had become visible, as one could read in a *Los Angeles Times* article titled "Koreans Pursue American Dream . . . and Find Land of Opportunity."[3] The Korean immigrant population, which had rapidly increased, worked hard and saved their incomes to open grocery stores, restaurants, dry cleaners, and other businesses. Amid the sluggish American economy of the 1970s, their success stories drew the attention of American society.

For the next two decades, Koreans worked to transform south LA, and Koreatown became as well-known as Chinatown and Little Tokyo. For immigrants, territorial identity held significant meaning in defining their existence within a society where they had restarted their lives but still felt like foreigners—too visible in their bodily appearance but too invisible in the formation of the society's meaning and values. In that society, Korean immigrants had not yet even reached the margin. The margin is understood as the opposite of the center. In order to recognize one's marginal position, one must be able to define oneself in relation to the center; thus, the margin requires its own identity.

But despite its seemingly individualistic connotation, identity is a communal concept. If an individual is not part of a community, they do not need or want to have an identity. A person's identity is defined in relation to that which is not their own. I am a woman, as opposed to being a man or nonbinary. If I were the only being on earth, I would not define myself as a woman; I would still *be* a woman, but what would be the point of defining myself as one if I were the only being on earth? Immigrants, in their earlier stages, have only a floating identity—and the name of that identity is survival.

In the case of Korean Americans, and for many immigrants in that context, attention-grabbing success stories and the floating identity of survival coexist as two sides of the same coin; society, however, will only see one of these sides. The missing link between the two sides is not easy to grasp. For Korean immigrants, there is often a second layer to the gap in their existence. Unlike professionals such as medical doctors, who might be able to find jobs related to their training in the United States, many Koreans who were well-educated and held office jobs in Korea had to give up their professions after arriving in this new world. Instead, they started small businesses like green grocery stores, dry cleaners, or laundromats—three of the most popular industries in which Koreans have found themselves working.

The gap between their position in South Korea and in the United States, in terms of social status—regardless of their financial capability—makes first-generation Korean Americans a kind of mystery to their children, the second-generation Korean Americans. The latter speak English as a native language and grew up immersed in American culture. For first-generation Korean Americans, Korean is their native language, which often makes them feel awkward when speaking English and navigating American cultural environments. The second-generation Korean Americans often view their parents—who spend all day, every day, working at a store—as having a narrow view of life. They often think their parents' lives solely revolve around making money. The Korean American writer Chang-rae Lee eloquently describes this relationship between the first- and second-generation Korean Americans and their search for identity in American society in his award-winning novel *Native Speaker* (1995).

The novel recounts the story of a second-generation Korean American named Henry, who grew up in New York City. Henry characterizes his father as "a Confucian of high order"[4] whose life "was all about money," saying his father "drew much energy and pride from his ability to make it almost at will. He was some kind of human annuity. He had no real cleverness or secrets for good business; he simply refused to fail."[5] His father, like many immigrants, "started with $200 in his pocket, a wife and baby, and just a few words of English,"[6] and eventually became the owner of several stores and "a majestic white house in Westchester," where he could "call himself a rich man."[7] This represents a typical Korean immigrant's success story, one might say.

When it comes to the material success of Korean immigrants—or, more broadly, of Asian immigrants—the story of Henry's father is not an isolated case. Since the late 1960s, the term "model minority" began to pervade the characterization of Asian Americans, who worked hard with perseverance, quietly and without resistance, conforming to social rules. They would work even in dangerous places in America's inner cities, amassing financial wealth and sending their children to prestigious universities. Some would argue that they are living proof that the American Dream is achievable and that America is a place of equal opportunity.

When the LA riots occurred, the media eagerly defined them as a Black-Korean conflict, even though the events themselves raised many unanswered questions about such a characterization. The "white problem" in American society was almost entirely evaded as the media focused on the narrative of Black Americans looting Korean stores on Olympic Boulevard and the image of a Korean man on a rooftop armed with a rifle. Meanwhile, the question of why Black Americans' rage against the racial injustice embodied by the acquittal of the white police officers—who had brutally beaten an African American man, with video of the incident so vividly highlighting the issue—failed to gain the attention it deserved.

In *Blue Dreams: Korean Americans and the Los Angeles Riots* (1995), the sociologists Nancy Abelmann and John Lie document the inappropriateness of using the label "Black–Korean conflict" to characterize the nature of the discord in the LA riots. "The majority of rioters and looters arrested were Latinos," they assert, not Black Americans or Korean Americans.[8] Given that many Latino Americans were working for Korean businesses, especially in Korean restaurants, it might make more sense to define the riots and lootings as a "Latino–Korean conflict," if we were to characterize the LA riots as an interethnic conflict. But the media repeatedly highlighted the frustrations of Black Americans, portraying their communities as plagued by broken families, alcohol addiction, and feelings of being defeated by Asian Americans, who were achieving noticeable financial success in America. Moreover, as Abelmann and Lie state, rioters and looters didn't intentionally avoid going to Beverly Hills and other white neighborhoods; they *couldn't* go to Beverly Hills because of the heavy police presence protecting that area. The media ignored this essential aspect of the incident's evolution.

The model minority theory served as a convenient device by which to justify the supposed existence of a Black-Korean conflict, which the media and white American society were overplaying through a monolithic interpretation of events that obscured the existence of racism in America. According to this narrative, Koreans were latecomers in the US immigration story, but they had already managed to achieve the American Dream through hard work in running their small businesses. While some Asian Americans might have achieved financial success this way, comparing their situation with that of other nonwhite Americans, such as African Americans, is like comparing apples to oranges. The fact is, as Abelmann and Lie clearly explain, Black Americans and Korean Americans were dealing with different conditions. Black Americans have been confronting transgenerational racism in the United States for centuries, whereas Korean Americans did not have such baggage and were able to focus on their business goals.

Like any categorization of an entire race of people, the model minority theory flattens the lives of Asian Americans into one homogeneous group of successful small business owners. Written immediately after the LA riots, *Blue Dreams* demonstrates the diversity of Korean Americans in terms of their financial status, jobs, and views on American society, revealing the false assumptions behind the model minority theory. For example, not all Korean Americans are small business owners, nor are they all successful entrepreneurs; there are impoverished Korean Americans as well as wealthy ones.

The model minority theory underemphasizes persistent anti–Asian American racism and implicitly criticizes other minorities, the authors assert. In sum, the model minority theory highlights a pivotal example of the perennial strategy that I call "placing minority against minority." By placing one minority group against another—in the case of the LA riots, Korean Americans against Black Americans—the model minority theory and the concept of Black-Korean conflict erase the main cause of all these social phenomena: racism, white supremacy, and social inequity in American society.

It is important to note that the model minority theory emerged in the late 1960s and early 1970s as a reaction to the civil rights movement, particularly from politically conservative Americans. During the 1960s, African American protests against American racism and discrimination were a critical element of the movement, which led conservatives to label Black Americans as "the problem minority." Before the emergence of the model minority theory, Asians were commonly referred to by the pejorative term "Orientals" and marked as "*definitively not-white.*"[9] White America had no doubt that Asians could never be placed in the same category as white Americans, or enjoy the privileges that whites did, no matter what. US policies like the Chinese Exclusion Act and the refusal to grant Asians eligibility for naturalization clearly demonstrated this mindset. But compared to "problem minorities"—namely, Black Americans— Asians were seen as the much-preferred choice. They were "politically nonthreatening, and *definitely not Black*"[10]; they were the "model minority." The questions of whose perspective defines Black Americans as "problem" minorities, and in what sense Asians are regarded as "model" minorities, require careful investigation to fully understand the intention behind these labels.

There is no positive categorization of racial groups. Categorization, by definition, requires conformity. If a woman is categorized as a "good girl," she is expected to conform to the requirements of what "good" means within that categorization. People often assume that being a "good girl" is part of that person's identity, but in reality, that cannot be the case. The concept of goodness, in this context, is defined by those who created the categorization, not by the individual herself, who should have a claim on her own identity. Similarly, when racial groups are categorized, those labels do not define the true nature or complexity of the individuals within them but instead enforce conformity to a constructed narrative.

If an individual is not the maker of their identity, that identity is only a name, not the reality of the person. In this sense, the modern Japanese thinker Nishida Kitaro defined identity as "absolute contradictory self-identity."[11] If we are to have an identity that separates ourselves from others, that identity cannot but be contradictory. Identity is not a static entity that we as individuals possess. In each and every moment, we act, and in Nishida's words, we constantly create identity through our own process of "making," using what has already been "made." A person encounters the world of the made, but the moment the world of the made is encountered by an individual, that person creates their own existence. I become myself by contradicting the ready-made identity of an Asian woman with the Asian woman who I become. This constant process of self-making equates to a constant awareness of the existence of others. We look at others in order to find our identity, just as we look in a mirror to check our appearance. The self, then, is possible not only because of the existence of others, but also because of an individual's own existence. Hence, absolute contradiction is the process through which we create our own individual self.

Everyone has a life they struggle to lead behind their simplified social and ideological categorizations—and that life is never monolithic. Henry's father in Lee's *Native Speaker* could serve as a good example of a successful

Korean American entrepreneur; he and his son Henry, or "his princely Hal,"[12] might be seen as representative model minorities. But their lives depicted in the novel are far from the static images of individuals in the model minority theory, which glorify the American Dream. Instead, their stories reveal the complexities, contradictions, and struggles that exist beyond these oversimplified categories, challenging the idealized narrative of success and assimilation. One reason such a flattening of life—better understood as discrimination—must be challenged is that it constitutes a kind of blasphemy: not against any deity, but against the sanctity of life, which can never be reduced to a simple definition. It affronts an individual's struggle to make sense of existence—which is, at best, absurd—derailing any efforts to find ultimate meaning.

In the novel, Henry later learns that his father, whom he had always known as a green grocery owner whose sole goal seemed to involve making money, was actually trained as an industrial engineer and had earned a master's degree at a top university in South Korea. Why did he come to the United States? Henry wondered. He could only speculate, based on hearsay, that without being connected to a "big network" or having societal connections, someone like his father, who came from a rural area, could not go far in Korean society. Once in the United States, he and Henry's mother planned to open a business, such as a green grocery store, and work day and night—all so their child who would speak fluent English and study hard could attend prestigious universities.

Many Korean storeowners in LA must have faced situations similar to that of Henry's father. But caught in the crossfire of the center's identity politics, which blamed both Black people and Koreans for the riots, Korean Americans who experienced the LA riots found themselves devastated. Having lost everything they had worked for during the years or even decades, they felt lost, unable to identify the true causes of their suffering or who should be held accountable for their tragedy. In a documentary film titled *Rodney King: Koreatown Reacts* (2016, directed by Christine Choy), a Korean liquor store owner named Yang Soon Han confessed, "I am angry at myself [because] I don't know to whom, to where should I be angry at. I am totally confused."[13] She had lost her store because of the riot. While Korean-Black conflict had emerged as an identifiable cause of the LA riots, the store owner understood that this conflict could not be the main cause of the situation, as the logic behind it simply did not add up.

In the aforementioned documentary, Guy Aoki, cofounder of the Media Action Network for Asian Americans, criticizes the media for exacerbating the conflict and turning it into a reality. He recounts what he heard from a member of his group: When a shooting occurred between a Chinese American store owner and a Black customer, the media showed no interest and refused to report the incident. But whenever anything happened between Black and Korean people, the media was sure to cover the story, often sensationalizing the situation. Aoki's critique highlights how media coverage played a significant role in amplifying tensions and creating a narrative that reinforced division between these communities.

The model minority theory depicts Asians' success not only as small business owners, but in educating their children at prestigious universities. Many second-generation Korean Americans must have wondered, especially as children, why their parents were so obsessed with education and prestigious universities. East Asian countries' zeal for education is well-known and has roots in the millennia-old Confucian tradition that emphasizes the value of education.

Confucians, or *rujia* in Chinese, were essentially scholars who were well-versed in classical texts that predated or were composed by Confucius (551–479 BCE), the founder of Confucianism. The first passage of Confucius's *Analects*, a record of his teachings, says: "To learn and practice what is learned every day, isn't this a pleasure?" For Confucians, learning is not just about acquiring information or skills; it is a process of training that shapes an individual into a true human being. Even today, many East Asian parents believe that excelling in school and earning a degree from a prestigious university is the "ticket" to success in life. There are complex reasons they believe this, but it was literally true in premodern Confucian society, because the civil service exam, which for centuries was used to select government officials in Korea and China, was based on the rote memorization of Confucian texts. Hence doing well in school, particularly in a Confucian academy, led directly to success by enabling a person to secure a position in public office.

Modernity gives this centuries-old practice an important twist. With the influx of Western culture and technology, Asian countries had to face the reality that their own value systems, cultures, and technological capacities were not on par with those of the West. As a result, they launched a race to catch up. The old traditions, such as Confucianism and Buddhism, could no longer present themselves as the primary sources of knowledge and values; instead,

Western philosophy, knowledge, science, and technology took their place. But the mindset persisted in which studying hard at school is a path to success.

For Korean Americans, turning hard work into tangible success often requires two generations of effort. The parents work to establish financial security for their children, and the children in turn study, attend elite schools, and secure professional jobs. The Confucian spirit of hard work and pursuit of a good job gained another twist when practiced in an American setting: the model minority theory. Working hard, as a deeply ingrained habit in traditional East Asian cultures, made Asian Americans ideal members of society by strengthening their capacity to weather the difficulties they faced as a minority group. But the fact that society would use this same trait to counter other ethnic groups was not a plan of Asians working in American society, whether of the first or the second generation.

Only as young adults do second-generation Korean Americans realize that they are not just Americans, but Korean- or Asian-Americans. The hyphen, when used to link ethnic or cultural identities, serves as more than a linguistic symbol; it signifies a tenacious and persistent connection between two worlds and two visions of life that influence almost every aspect of their existence. Their identity hangs between Korea/Asia and the United States, forever changing, forever challenged, belonging completely to neither but aspiring to belong to both.

Native Speaker depicts the ambiguous position that Asian Americans occupy in the grand narrative of American society. The author positions Henry, the protagonist, as a private detective—a figure whose identity cannot be revealed and is constantly in flux depending on the situation. This choice is a symbolic statement of the impossibility Asian Americans face in assuming a permanent, visible, and presentable identity.

Henry's desperate aspiration to fit into American society leads to his fascination with the public figure John Kwang, a Korean American running for mayor of New York, who to Henry, seems to be "effortlessly Korean, effortlessly American." This stands in stark contrast to Henry's own father, whose life is confined to his greengrocer's shop and his limited English. At the end of the novel, however, John Kwang is revealed to be embroiled in money laundering and drunk driving, not the true public leader or father figure that Henry had hoped to find. Fully disillusioned, Henry observes:

> I felt alone, alarmingly so. And washing the sleep from my face, I remembered how for a time in my boyhood I would often awake before dawn and step outside on the front porch. It was always perfectly quiet and dark, as if the land were completely unpeopled save for me. No Korean father or mother, no taunting boys or girls, no teachers showing me how to say my American name. I'd then run back inside and look in the mirror, desperately hoping in that solitary moment to catch a glimpse of who I truly was; but looking back at me was just the same boy again, no clearer than before, unshakably lodged in that difficult face.[14]

The success story of Asian Americans and the model minority theory that spotlights this success ignore the various challenges that Asian Americans endure with their hyphenated identity in white American society. Rather than leading people to understand the agony of those at the margin and improve their living conditions, the model minority theory has been used to pit minority against minority. With this strategy, the center controls the margins by blaming them for the problems that the center and the margin both suffer from, thereby evading responsibility for those issues. The "minorities," or those at the margin, however, are not homogeneous groups with solid and definable identities. An individual's identity might seem to be defined by something visible or even tangible, such as a "yellow" Asian face, dark skin, a woman's bodily contours, or even publicly invisible but assumed reproductive organs. But beyond and behind that visible and assumed identity lies a chimera called life, with its unfathomable depth and complexity.

Henry's search for identity obviously does not apply only to Asian Americans. Every individual must undergo their own search for identity and find the meaning of existence in their own way, with their own problems and limitations, and with whatever capacities they possess to cope with them. The model minority theory deprives individuals of the basic ecology of existence by flattening their beings, all for the benefit of the center. The strategy of pitting minority against minority functions because society allows such flattening, which itself is a form of violence.

Race and ethnicity are not the only realms in which the strategy of setting minority against minority has proven its usefulness. The patriarchal system has camouflaged its unfair gender practices for centuries by pitting minority against minority. The common conflict between mothers-in-law and daughters-in-law in Confucian society is a good example of this. In Korean society, this tension, conflict, and hostility has driven countless women's lives to hell.

The patriarchal nature of the Confucian tradition is well documented. Scholars have traced its origins back to pre-Confucian texts in Chinese intellectual history, such as the *Book of Changes*. Confucius's own remarks on women have often been noted: "Women and inferior men are most difficult to deal with. If you are familiar with them, they cease to be humble. If you keep a distance from them, they resent it."[15] The expression "inferior men" here refers to people who are the opposite of the ideally cultivated person in the Confucian tradition—the "superior man." Thus in this passage, Confucius is equating women with the worst kind of men. Some scholars have argued that in the language of his time, the term translated as "women" actually referred not to adult women[16] but only to little girls. But the argument is not particularly convincing, especially given the enduring influence of the statement on East Asian society throughout history.

Mencius, the second best known figure in the Confucian tradition and one credited with establishing classical Confucian philosophy, defined the code of conduct for women unambiguously: "At the marriage of a young woman, her mother instructs her. She accompanies the daughter to the door on her leaving and admonishes her, saying, 'Go to your home. Always be respectful and careful. Never disobey your husband.' Thus, to regard obedience as the correct course of conduct is the way for women."[17]

Mencius lived during the third century BCE, and for more than two millennia his idea of obedience to men as a prime virtue of women did not lose its power. Once an ideological "prime directive" like this is established, various logistical structures are employed to make it work in people's daily lives. One ensuing phenomenon was the competitive and often hostile relationship between mothers-in-law and daughters-in-law in Korean society.

Confucianism came to Korea early in its history, perhaps around the fourth century. But many scholars today note that the actual Confucianization of Korea took place much later—sometime around the eighteenth century, according to JaHyun Kim Haboush, a scholar of Korean Confucianism.[18] This does not mean that Confucianism didn't affect Korean society before that time. But the social practices of Confucianism as we know them today, such as its patriarchal, patrilocal, and patrilineal aspects, were firmly established as customs in Korean society only around the eighteenth century, according to Haboush.

In Confucian Korea, a household is recorded as a family lineage that identifies members according to the patrilineal system: the line runs from father to son, and daughters are included in their natal family's record only temporarily, to be removed once they marry. As Mencius stated, a woman's "home" is with her husband's family, not her birth family. As an outsider the woman's only connection to her "real home" is thus her husband: he is the source of her identity. Her identity as a wife also includes her role as a daughter-in-law, an outsider who is a provisional member of the family. The only way for the woman to become a "real" member of the family is to give birth to a male child who is a real member of the family from the moment he is born. If the woman fails to produce a male child, she risks being removed from the family.

For this reason, a male child can be even more important than a husband in a woman's life in Confucian society, as only a son guarantees her permanent position in her husband's family. When this son grows up and gets married, he is both the son to his mother and the husband to his wife. A triangular relationship is inevitable, since for both women, this man is their only connection to their family, the only source of identity and belonging. As a result, the women constantly compete for his attention, and the tension between them escalates.

This conflict between mother-in-law and daughter-in-law has often been portrayed as stemming from undesirable aspects of femininity: jealousy, distrust, lying, conspiracy, and so on. These traits are also depicted as petty characteristics of women, in contrast to the generous minds of men who try to stay away from the feud. This centuries-old tradition masks the root of the problem: the patriarchal system maintained by the central power of men, setting minority against minority and blaming the margin as the source of the tension and hostility. The fact that the patriarchal system is the foundational cause of the mother-in-law and daughter-in-law conflict does not diminish the struggles women face. The other woman—whether mother-in-law or daughter-in-law—becomes the immediate cause of a woman's pain and tragedy, while the real cause, the patriarchal system, is effectively hidden behind the scenes.

Understanding the structure of discrimination, such as the strategy of pitting minority against minority, may not radically diminish the suffering of people in marginalized positions. This reflection can nevertheless help us view the problem from a multidimensional perspective, clarify

MINORITY AGAINST MINORITY

obscure dimensions of racism and patriarchy, and educate those on the margins on how to address the problems rather than simply accepting their situation as fate or blaming the margin itself on the basis of the center's narrative. This strategy of setting minority against minority is a divide-and-conquer tactic. But it reveals the underlying structure of this approach and can be applied to other forms of conflict where the root causes may be hidden beneath other problems.

The paradigm of the center pitting minority against minority to control the margins and sustain its own power does not mean that minorities are all innocent victims. In the case of the so-called Black–Korean conflict, both Koreans and Blacks played roles. Korean merchants were frequently criticized for their mistreatment of Black customers, but they also lived in constant anxiety knowing they were doing business in an unsafe area. Despite the risks, they set up their businesses there because their limited resources prevented them from competing with white middle class businesses.

If we were to say that the minorities were purely victims here, we would also deny their agency, their ability to act in accord with their own will. They did act, but the agency of marginalized groups must be understood within the social structures that surround them: What are the parameters of agency for a minority group living with limited capacity? This brings us to the importance of society in directing the agency of marginalized groups. If a society envisions a future in which people in disadvantaged positions have opportunities to overcome their marginalization, it must address the structural injustices that keep people trapped in those circumstances. The model minority theory—or the idea of "problem minorities"—demonstrates the opposite. Instead of creating opportunities for marginalized groups to gain equal footing with the privileged, these ideologies diminish what capacity the marginalized group have in order to justify and enhance the power of the center.

By proposing "minority against minority" as a strategy the center uses to control the margins, I want to draw attention to a political dimension of our awareness and subsequent engagement with society. By "political" I do not mean only activities of politics and activism. Politics, by definition, is related to a "polis," a community. When feminists began claiming that "the personal is political," it was an invitation to rethink the meaning and scope of our daily activities. An individual lives within a community, is a part of it, and their personal actions take place in the context of that community. Therefore, these actions are political in the sense that they have an impact on both that individual and other members of the community.

The twentieth-century Chinese thinker Zhao Tingyang defined politics as "the communal art of living" and the political as "the creative art of coexistentiality for everyone involved, . . . the art of transforming the spaces of conflictual competition into a world of shared coexistence."[19] These definitions can sound idealistic, especially in our time, when politics is often more about criticizing those who belong to different political parties or who disagree with us, rather than about living together with them. But precisely because of this, Zhao's definition challenges us to reflect on what the political truly involves, and why it should be this way. If we do not wish to live together with others, we do not need to engage politically. But even when we strive to coexist with others, important questions must be asked about who is included among these "others," and how we go about positioning ourselves in relation to them.

Scholars have pointed out that the victim narrative of Korean Americans, which defined the LA riots as merely a Black–Korean conflict, not only misrepresents the situation but also renders Korean Americans as bystanders without agency. If the model minority theory strips Asian Americans of their agency by imposing a wholesale characterization on them, the idea of minority-against-minority reveals the consequences of such sweeping simplification of the lives of individuals within the group.

There were sociopsychological elements to the LA riots and the Black–Korean relationship as well. Despite being represented as a "model minority," Koreans and Asian Americans in general are often treated as foreigners because of their physical visibility, regardless of how many generations they have lived there. By contrast, from the perspective of Korean Americans, Black Americans are typically considered fully American despite the history of slavery, suppression of voting rights, and other systemic barriers. This reflects the complex dynamics of race and identity in the United States, which played a large role in shaping the interactions between these communities during the riots.

One incident often cited as fueling Black anger toward Korean Americans and thus used to explain the LA riots as a Black–Korean conflict, was the death of fifteen-year-old Latasha Hirlins in March 1991, a year before the riots. Hirlins was fatally shot by Soon Ja Du, a Korean convenience store owner who accused Hirlins of stealing a bottle of orange juice. Soon Ja Du was convicted of voluntary manslaughter but served no jail time; she was sentenced to five

MINORITY AGAINST MINORITY

years of probation, four-hundred hours of community service, and a $500 fine. This sentence enraged the Black
community, who saw it as an injustice. Hirlins's family
members continue to pursue justice for her. This raises
several questions: What would justice for Hirlins involve?
Would it mean revisiting the sentencing and demanding a
heavier punishment? How should she be remembered
thirty years after her death?

The nineteen-minute documentary *A Love Song for Latasha* (2019) offers valuable perspectives on these questions.
The film shows viewers who Latasha was and what she
dreamed of for her life through narration by her friends
and family members. It reveals how, in Latasha's words,
"dangerous, ruthless, uncaring people" mistreated her and
her community; yet there is no mention of Korean Americans or a Black–Korean conflict. The film, as the title
makes explicit, focuses on Latasha Hirlins as a person: an
individual who lived life like anyone else, with dreams and
plans for her future, not defined solely by her tragic death
over a $1.75 bottle of orange juice.

In a discussion after the screening of the film, director
Sophia Nahli Allison never mentioned the Black–Korean
conflict. Even the video footage of Du shooting Latasha to
death doesn't appear in the film; the incident is represented with digitalized symbolic images. When asked
about her decision not to show the "evidence" of the killing, Allison explained that she couldn't allow Latasha's
family, friends, and community to relive that trauma. She
felt that she couldn't make the Black community continue
to witness their bodies covered in blood. She observed,
"We don't need to see the death to validate why the person's life was so important."[20] Her words magnificently

challenge the way we memorialize the dead and find meaning in their deaths, especially a violent and wrongful death. By choosing not to focus explicitly on violence, Allison shifts the narrative from one of victimhood to one of humanity and dignity, urging us to reflect on the life that was lived rather than on the circumstances of its end. This approach invites a more respectful and thoughtful way of remembering the deceased, one that transcends the trauma and acknowledges the complexity of the person's existence.

When traumatic incidents like the death of Latasha Hirlins, the beating of Rodney King, and the LA riots occur, we repeatedly revisit the appalling moments, the crime scenes. It is important to know what happened. But just as important as finding "evidence" of the crimes is remembering the people who died. The way we recall and honor their lives, their humanity, and their dreams can shape the way we understand their deaths and the larger social issues surrounding them. By focusing on their identities beyond their tragic deaths, we not only pay tribute to their memories but challenge the reductive narratives that might define them solely as victims. Mourning is an act of remembrance and should not be treated as part of an investigation into a crime.

Earlier I discussed grievability and how its nature and scope vary with the social standing of the deceased. The dead are remembered, and the living keep those memories alive and shape the grief for the dead. The living are memory keepers, and how and what kinds of memories they preserve is up to them. It is one thing to revisit a scene of death; it is another to learn the person's life story. This is an occasion to reaffirm the importance of what I call "narrative philosophy."[21] Everyone deserves to be understood in a holistic way, through the story of their entire life, rather than being reduced to a single incident, no matter how defining.

In the same discussion, Allison asked why people still talk about Rodney King while Latasha Hirlins has almost been forgotten. A similar question was posed in the documentary *Vincent Who?* (2009). In that film, director Tony Lam asked eighty young Asian Americans whether they had heard of Vincent Chin, and all of them responded in the negative. As the title reveals, the common response was something along the lines of, "Vincent who?" Vincent Chin, a Chinese American man in his late twenties, was killed in 1982 outside a bar in Michigan by two white men he had had an argument with. The men followed Vincent outside and hit him with a baseball bat while using racial slurs. Vincent went into a coma and died four days later. The men, Ronald Ebens, a Chrysler plant supervisor, and his stepson Michael Nitz, a laid-off autoworker, had assumed that Vincent was Japanese and were taking out their anger at the Japanese auto industry, which they blamed for the loss of American automobile jobs. The two men were charged with manslaughter and sentenced to three years of probation and a $3,000 fine, but they did not serve any time in jail. The Asian American community was enraged by the lenient sentence.

Several individuals in *Vincent Who?* do remember him and reflect on how Vincent Chin's death served as a pivotal moment for Asian Americans, awakening a collective consciousness. Before the incident, distinct communities existed of Chinese Americans, Japanese Americans, and Korean Americans, but no unified identity of "Asian

American" had emerged. The term had been in use since the late 1960s, but its meaning was still evolving. Vincent Chin's death galvanized Asian Americans and brought them to see themselves as a distinct marginalized group within American society. It thus marked a turning point in the development of their shared identity and political awareness.

Simply being on the margin does not make one a marginal being. For the margin to be recognized as such, it must be able to define itself in relation to the center, and an awareness of this relationship between the two must emerge. People of Chinese and Japanese descent had been living in the United States since the mid-nineteenth century, yet the collective identity of Asian Americans did not exist then. African Americans existed since the founding of the United States, and Indigenous peoples lived on the land before the Declaration of Independence. It was only through the recognition of their historical contexts and struggles that groups began to define themselves more clearly, not just in relation to their own histories, but to the broader social and political structures of American society.

Yet considering all these minority groups together in their marginal situation might be a relatively new practice. The *New York Times* columnist Jay Caspian Kang, in his book *The Loneliest Americans* (2022), reflects: "When we were kids, if someone had told me that Dwayne [an African American classmate of his] and I were both 'minorities' or had some shared experiences as 'people of color,' I would have looked at him like he had lost his mind."[22] I trust that this is no longer a common perspective. As awareness of shared struggles and experiences has grown, the notion of a collective minority identity has evolved, fostering a broader understanding of solidarity among marginalized groups.

What would it look like to bring together different minority groups in the context of marginality, uniting their voices in a collective effort to challenge discrimination and inequity? What steps need to be taken for marginalized communities to find the strength to confront the center, whose power far surpasses their own? How might solidarity within the margins be cultivated to empower communities to take that path? In the next and final chapter I delve into these complex and essential questions.

5

Reflexive Engagement

Three students sat at the back of the classroom, seemingly settled into the spots they had chosen at the semester's start. With nearly a third of the term gone, they were all falling behind on their assignments and hadn't engaged in class activities. What was going on with them? the woman wondered. Maybe it was time for her to step in and remind them that they needed to keep up with their work if they expected to pass the course.

"Are you aware you're behind on your homework?" she asked. "Why aren't you engaging in class?"

The three boys exchanged glances, possibly weighing whether to be honest, deflect the question, make a false promise to catch up, or respond with frustration.

"Why do we have to complete nine credits of college English when college Korean is only three credits?" one of them asked. "We're Koreans. We should be taking more Korean courses than English."

The students felt compelled to challenge the university's requirement to complete three courses in college

English but only one in Korean. The curriculum was a product of American imperialism, they argued. At the time, anti-American sentiment was strong in South Korea, alongside widespread demonstrations against the military government.[1] Many Koreans, including the students in that class, viewed the United States as a supporter of South Korea's authoritarian government, which had been suppressing freedom, violating democratic principles, and committing violence against its own citizens in events like the Gwangju Uprising.

The woman responded by quoting *The Art of War* by Sun Tzu, a Chinese classic from the fifth century BCE: "Sun Tzu teaches that if you know your enemy and engage in battle, you will win every time; but if you don't understand your enemy and fight, you will lose every time. If your goal is to challenge American imperialism, you must first master English and use it as a tool in your struggle. Boycotting your English class will only result in an F, which does nothing to further your fight against imperialism."

This incident occurred during my first semester teaching at the college level, when I was an adjunct lecturer in my twenties. The students seemed to be persuaded by my argument, gradually engaging more and eventually completing all their assignments. Decades later, I still wonder whether the logic I offered truly makes sense. Sun Tzu's reasoning seems sound, but is it true that to fight against imperialism, one must learn the imperialist language? Can one learn a language without internalizing its culture? If the margin adopts the language and culture of the center, can it still challenge the center without being co-opted? On the other hand, if the margin refuses to learn the language and culture of the center, what tools does it have to confront and destabilize the center and make its own voices heard? Can the margin invent a new language, one that is its own? And if it does, would the center seek to understand it without prematurely dismissing it?

These questions have undoubtedly been asked countless times as postcolonial discourses emerged and long before, when marginalized groups have tried to prove their worth to the center, or even simply to survive. The margins have at times erupted in revolts, submitted petitions to governments, marched in civil disobedience, and written about the harsh realities they endure. How do people envision a new world, a new society, and a new life when their environment constantly undervalues their existence, and their lives seem to be controlled by invincible forces? Is resistance even possible? If so, what form does it take? In this final chapter, I invite the reader to reflect not only on the possibility of the margin's efforts to survive, but on how the margin creates its own values and meanings, and how it can become a force for social change. In that context, we must also consider how we can reconceptualize the relationship between the margin and the center, seeking a deeper understanding of their dynamic interplay.

The postcolonial thinker and anticolonial activist Frantz Fanon (1925–1961) argued that to counter the violence of colonizers, colonized people are compelled to use violence in the process of decolonization. Born in the French colony of Martinique, Fanon earned a psychiatry degree in France and then went to Africa to practice, where his experiences deeply influenced his writings on colonialism, violence, and liberation.

In *The Wretched of the Earth* (1961), published shortly after his untimely death from leukemia, Fanon

unwaveringly describes the exploitation of natives by set-
tlers whose logic is rooted in a compartmentalized, Mani-
chean, dualistic worldview. In the colonial world, everything is divided into two categories with a clear hierarchy:
not just power and wealth, but the physical structures of
residential areas, buildings, and even values. This rigid
division reinforces the supremacy of the colonizers and
the subjugation of the colonized, perpetuating the structures of inequality and violence. Fanon describes the set-
tler's distorted sense of values: "Native society is not simply described [by the settlers] as a society lacking in
values. . . . The native is declared insensible to ethics; he
represents not only the absence of values, but also the
negation of values. He is . . . the enemy of values, and in
this sense, he is the absolute evil."[2]

In the colonial world, power and wealth dictate what is
valued and what is considered right: those who hold power
determine values and define morality. Although the world
may have moved beyond the colonialism that dominated
the late nineteenth and early twentieth centuries, the align-
ment of power and wealth with values persists and has
even intensified in our time. Fanon argued that the colonized must resort to violence in response to the relentless
violence used by colonizers to control them. He believed
that under the oppression of colonial violence, the colonized are weak and powerless, and that only by countering
the colonizer's violence with violence can they hope to win.
"The native's violence unifies people,"[3] he wrote in *The
Wretched Earth*. "The practice of violence binds [the colo-
nized] together as a whole,"[4] and "the colonized man finds
his freedom in and through violence."[5]

118

Despite his strong support for violence as a tool for colonized peoples' liberation, Fanon did not promote violence unconditionally. He argued that violence should be used only as part of the decolonizing process. Once the colonized are liberated, they must rebuild their society, and this task cannot be accomplished through violence. Fanon's proposal raises important questions: At what point can we say decolonization is complete? Does it end with a declaration of independence? Postcolonial reality reveals that decolonization does not simply occur on the day of independence. It is a prolonged process, because the colonizer's world—its language, culture, and thought—has deeply permeated the lives of the colonized people. Despite these unresolved questions, *The Wretched of the Earth* is repeatedly cited as endorsing the use of violence by colonized and oppressed peoples in their struggles.

Yet the vision Fanon proposed at the end of his book is often overlooked. He concluded with an image of a "new man" who will break free of Europe and create a new world. "We must turn over a new leaf, we must work out new concepts, and try to set afoot a new man,"[6] he urged his readers. "Let us try to create the whole man, whom Europe has been incapable of bringing to triumphant birth."[7] I doubt that this new man, this whole man that Fanon envisioned, would be one to repeat the violence of old Europe—the tool of the colonizers. If a new world is to be built and a new being is to be born, violence must be transcended. The compartmentalized, bifurcated worldview, which is a legacy of colonial Europe and a root cause of violence, must be transformed. But Fanon didn't spell out what the birth of this new whole man would involve.

What procedure, what kind of transformation, would facilitate the shift from the violent old world to a new one? If he had lived, his next book might have explored the specifics of this process. But we don't have that book, having lost Fanon at age thirty-six.

According to Fanon, the colonizer's dehumanization leaves the colonized people with little choice except to resort to violence themselves to counter the power of the center. A similar dynamic can be observed in the relationship between different social classes in a capitalist society. *A Dwarf Launches a Little Ball*, a novel I discussed in chapter 3, highlights the inhumane treatment of factory workers by capitalists during the early stages of modernization in South Korea. This treatment, much like the colonial dynamic, fosters an environment where the marginalized are pushed toward resistance in response to the business owner's exploitation.

After being evicted from their house, the family eventually move to an industrial complex where all three children find factory jobs with long working hours, at less than minimum wage and with inhumane treatment. The factories consistently ignore or suppress efforts by workers to unionize or even to address their poor working conditions and inadequate compensation. Eventually, the eldest son, Yŏngsu, concludes that there is no way to make their voices heard other than through violence. He plans to kill the head of the group that owns the factories but, because of their similar appearances, he mistakenly kills the owner's brother. For this he is sentenced to death and executed. The story seems to suggest that for workers, violence is the only path to raise their voices, even if it comes at the cost of their lives.

The novel does not end there, though. Like Fanon, who proposed leaving old Europe with its violence and anticipated the emergence of a new man, the author of *A Dwarf Launches a Little Ball* includes a brief epilogue involving a math teacher—a framing figure who appears at both the beginning and end of the novel—declaring to his graduating students that he would like to travel to a distant planet and live with extraterrestrial beings. He also tells his students to remember, "Whether you live on Earth or on another planet, our mind is always free."[8] This is a rather enigmatic statement to digest after more than three hundred pages about struggling factory workers and their families who live below the poverty line and endure inhumane treatment in a capitalist society. Freedom was not part of their lives, neither the freedom to act according to their will nor freedom from oppression. What does the author suggest by ending the novel with a character expressing such conviction about the possibility of freedom?

In searching for an answer, I turn here to the novel's title: *A Dwarf Launches a Little Ball*. In the story, the dwarf father launches a paper airplane toward the moon from the top of a chimney. This act symbolizes his resistance to the society that has humiliated him and his family, and it represents his way of exercising freedom. Will the paper airplane have any impact on society? The idea seems absurd. But literary devices often carry their own messages, and this one expresses the necessity of action and engagement. It suggests that each individual must participate to prove their existence and create meaning in their life. No matter how small each action seems, engagement and resistance are essential for declaring the value of an

121

individual's existence. In this sense, the story ends with a message of hope, even if it appears as tiny as the light emitted by a firefly.

Yeong-hye, the main character of *The Vegetarian*, another novel I discussed in chapter 3, is taken to the emergency room at the end of the third story in the trilogy. Her life is in danger because she refuses to eat following her realization that human existence is inevitably entangled with violence, and that she herself has been both its perpetrator and its victim. She claims that she wants to become a tree: a living thing that does not need to commit violence against others for its own survival. On one hand, Yeong-hye's refusal to eat can be seen as her inflicting violence on herself, as it puts her life at risk. On the other hand, her story represents an extreme way of imagining resistance to violence, by envisioning beings that can survive only through photosynthesis—an existence free from the violence that is inherent in human survival.

Fanon's new man who would leave Europe and create a world without violence, the dwarf father launching a paper airplane to attain freedom, and Yeong-hye's determination to become a plant in order to survive without violence—none of these proposals might seem practical. But proposing a vision neither guarantees a real solution to the problem nor ensures its success. Instead, it signifies an awareness of the inevitability of action. Proposing a vision is an acknowledgment that, in the face of systemic violence and oppression, some form of resistance or engagement is necessary, even if the outcome is uncertain or the methods unconventional. This awareness also involves, as Judith Butler emphasized in her discussion of nonviolence, a constant and consistent struggle. The visions listed above speak to the power of possibility. No one can say that they will be realized, but no one can say that they won't. The urgency of existential and social reality propels the power of possibility and the inevitability of action.

In Buddhism, this awareness and the exercise of the inevitability of action are embodied in compassion, which is considered one of Buddhism's two wings, the other being wisdom. Wisdom, or *prajñā* in Sanskrit, is a technical term in Buddhism. It refers to cognitive insight that is free from personal biases and preferences, enabling an individual to see the world as it truly is. This type of wisdom has the capacity to lead to enlightenment. Wisdom also refers to the inherent quality of an enlightened being. One important aspect of East Asian Buddhism is how it holds that the quality of an enlightened being is not exclusive to a special group of people. Rather, East Asian Buddhism teaches that we all have the capacity for enlightenment. Therefore, we should look within ourselves to realize this potential and free ourselves from a biased view of the world.

From the moment we are born and even before birth, through biological imprints, we constantly accumulate experiences, knowledge, ideas, views, and values. The totality of these elements forms an individual's personality, character, and life. In our capitalist society, accumulation is prized. Both the accumulation of wealth and the accumulation of knowledge are seen as demonstrations of success in life. By contrast, Buddhism views accumulation as an obstacle. As we accumulate wealth, we become more susceptible to greed. Similarly, as we accumulate knowledge, there is a risk of developing a more biased view of things and others. Buddhism encourages people to envision "ground zero"—not in the sense of returning to the state before birth, but as an understanding of beings before they are reinterpreted through the lens of the subject's accumulated preferences.

Value judgments are an inherent part of human existence, and their formation largely depends on what value system we adopt and adapt through socialization. In Buddhist terminology, efforts to reach ground zero are efforts to realize emptiness, which is equivalent to wisdom. As I have mentioned several times, the Buddhist worldview posits that things exist through causes and conditions, not as a result of a permanent essence. "Emptiness" is another expression of this state of identity. Things and beings are "empty" of a permanent, enduring essence and "full" of everything. Buddhist wisdom is an awareness of this emptiness, which is directly linked to the practice of compassion.

The Buddhist teachings about the capacity for enlightenment and the concept of emptiness may sound too abstract. But when placed in the context of the ultimate goal of Buddhism, which is to eliminate suffering, these ideas may not seem as alien. Frustration, despair, and pain often stem from unfulfilled desires and expectations. The ability to examine the complex causes of an event and acknowledge our stubborn reluctance to accept reality, especially when it doesn't align with our preferences, is the first step toward freeing ourselves from negative emotions and mental struggle. Buddhism asserts that this transformation in an individual not only liberates them from unnecessary suffering but also leads them to help others achieve the same state.

In the Buddhist paradigm, an enlightened being demonstrates the characteristic of wisdom and exercises this wisdom through compassion. But what about the innumerable individuals who have yet to attain enlightenment? In contemporary Buddhist discourse, the concept of Buddhist awakening or enlightenment has often been inflated, as if reaching that goal is the sole purpose of Buddhist practice. In this context, Dale S. Wright, a scholar of Chinese Buddhism, suggests that we use the expression "the thought of enlightenment" rather than simply saying "enlightenment" to shift our understanding of these ideas.

Buddhist enlightenment or awakening is often understood as a final goal, a perspective that has been heavily influenced by the goal-oriented modern world. If Buddhist practice were solely about achieving enlightenment, the story of Gautama Siddhartha, the founder of Buddhism, would end at age thirty-five, when he is said to have attained awakening. What more could there be to say after he had achieved his goal? Yet, Buddhist literature contains extensive accounts of his activities and teachings throughout his lifetime. Whether these accounts hold historical value as "facts" or are products of religious imagination, it is clear that the majority of Buddhist teachings focus on the Buddha's life *after* his enlightenment rather than on the event of his enlightenment itself.

Consider how many people in the more than 2,500-year history of Buddhism might have attained enlightenment. While no one has statistics on this, it's obvious that only a very small number of individuals have reached that stage. If that is the case, why talk about enlightenment at all? And how receptive would people be to practicing a form of Buddhism that emphasizes compassion and wisdom—the qualities of the enlightened being—when most practitioners have yet to attain awakening and the chance of reaching that state seems so infinitesimal?

Buddhist tradition, however, has emphasized wisdom and compassion throughout its history. The "thought of enlightenment" does not simply entail thinking about enlightenment, nor does it suggest that enlightenment is a single point in time or a final goal. Instead, it offers guidance toward our freedom to shape the kind of life we will lead—which is, as Wright puts it, "the primary responsibility and opportunity that human beings have."[9] This suggests that enlightenment should be understood as a continuous process rather than a final goal. And the effort to move toward enlightenment and freedom is called cultivation.

Life continues. Life is a process, and no single moment, however magnificent, can replace the duration of a being's life. In discussing the importance of duration in the context of postmodern ethics, the philosopher David Wood offers the example of having a great lunch. Suppose a person had a fantastic lunch today. However wonderful that lunch was, it cannot replace all of the lunches the person will have to eat each day for the rest of their life. But the memory and impact of that great lunch will change the quality of their life. A great lunch might not be the best comparison to the seemingly serious and weighty concepts of enlightenment and practice. But the effort to move toward enlightenment and freedom, which we call cultivation, also requires persistence in improving ourselves and living out our lives. It is not an action that can take place once and then be automatically maintained.

The Buddhist idea of wisdom can be compared to the current discourse on epistemic justice. Earlier I discussed the concept of epistemic injustice, which occurs when a statement is judged not by its content but by the speaker's social position. The wisdom that Buddhism promotes is related to practicing epistemic justice, in which statements and actions are understood without being distorted by the position or disposition of either the speaker or the listener.

Buddhist cultivation, among other aspects, involves a process of self-reflection on our behaviors and decision-making. The core of this reflection lies in discerning whether an action will contribute to suffering or alleviate it. This reflective process acknowledges the complex causal chain in which both the decision-maker and the individuals or entities affected by their decisions are situated. The impact of our actions is not limited to ourselves but extends to the broader web of relationships and circumstances that may be influenced by those choices.

Buddhism asserts that, by reorienting our value systems to account for both our own suffering and that of others, we can begin to reconceptualize the nature of existence. Unlike moral systems that are grounded in a categorical imperative, Buddhist teachings are not prescriptive in the sense of an absolute obligation. Buddhism does not claim that we *ought* to practice it. Instead, it operates through a hypothetical imperative: if we seek to alleviate suffering, we should consider the path of Buddhist practice. In this sense, Buddhism approaches ethics from a perspective that differs significantly from the one that posits the categorical imperative as the foundation of moral action. Why is that the case? What would be the benefit and efficacy of using "suffering" as a measure for any moral and ethical action, rather than establishing inviolable rules as the foundation of ethics?

What if someone does not think that suffering is part of their life and believes that their life is going well? In that case, Buddhism would say that Buddhism is of no use to

127

that person. One audacious assumption of the Buddhist tradition is that everyone will encounter moments when suffering becomes a profound part of their existence. This assumption is not difficult to grasp. Everyone gets sick from time to time; everyone grows old, and aging is not one of the exciting aspects of life for most people. Ultimately, everyone must face death. Between birth and death, people experience various forms of struggle, both materially and mentally. Suffering is an inherent part of existence. When Buddhism focuses on suffering, the intention is not to view existence through a pessimistic lens. Rather, Buddhism emphasizes cultivating the capacity to face and understand suffering, which enables individuals to navigate through suffering and live more meaningfully.

128

Some of us might recall the strangely beautiful experience of recovering from a serious illness. Even after being bedridden with something as simple as a seasonal cold, when our energy slowly returns and we take our first steps away from the bed, the sunlight suddenly feels and looks so different. The once-common sight of sunlight streaming through the window now evokes a sense of awe, through which we marvel at the beauty of the light and the sheer wonder of being alive. At that moment, we feel as if we could love any being, perhaps even forget any negative feelings we're holding, and simply be content to exist surrounded by the world. This could be a moment when personal desires fade and the mind resets, free from its accumulated biases and knowledge. In such a moment, we're not at the center of the world; rather, it is the sense of being together—with the sunlight and with anyone or any other beings we are with—that brings the beauty of being alive.

Buddhist practice encourages us to continually return to these moments of fresh perception, viewing the world with new eyes.

The Buddha did not use the term "marginality," but the connection between Buddhist practice and the concept of marginality is clear. As we know, Gautama Siddhartha was a prince in a tribe in what is now northern India, near present-day Nepal. Eventually, he renounced his privileged position and journeyed into the wilderness of India to seek the meaning of existence. "Leaving home," a term used in Korean to describe joining the monastery, signifies renouncing all worldly possessions. Traditionally, Buddhist monastics were homeless individuals who survived by begging. In fact, begging is one of the oldest practices in Buddhism. In a modern industrial society, however, the image of a homeless person, or more specifically, a beggar, carries various connotations, often raising concerns about hygiene and mental illness. In Buddhist tradition, homelessness is an intentional effort that places us in the lowest position, to the extent that we must beg for food, the essential element of survival. But being homeless or houseless is distinct from being a beggar. Being houseless refers to the lack of ownership of a permanent dwelling, whereas being a beggar means relying on the mercy or generosity of others for sustenance.

Being a beggar means occupying the lowest possible position in the spectrum of living conditions, at the very margin of society. The traditional Buddhist practice of begging led its followers to live on the margins and seek the meaning of existence there while also helping others. Begging was not merely a practice of humility; it also provided an opportunity for others to accumulate merit by donating to the begging monastics. Begging, however, carries a completely different meaning in our time. At the beginning of the modern period, the Korean reform-minded Buddhist monk Han Yongun (1879–1944) called for the abolition of this practice, which he saw as making Buddhist monastics live as parasites in modern society. He urged monastics to engage in productive work, suggesting that they join a production line. While the way marginality is practiced may evolve over time, the underlying teaching of begging remains relevant. Buddhist practice, with its focus on alleviating suffering, should remain grounded in understanding and helping those who are at the margins of society.

Buddhism is not unique among religious traditions in offering teachings about being at and practicing from the margin. Jung Young Lee, a Korean American theologian, interpreted Jesus Christ and Christianity through the lens of marginality. Critical of Christians who eagerly strive to occupy the center of society, Lee argues that "Jesus' public ministry may best be characterized as a life of marginality. He was a homeless man, surrounded by a group of homeless people, and none of his disciples came from 'the religious political establishment.'"[10] Jesus's marginality, Lee explains, was divinely ordained, as God chose for him to be born in the humblest of places, a stable, and as an outcast. For Lee, the birth of Jesus and thus Christmas represent "Jesus' divine marginalization: God marginalized his Son to save the world."[11] But Jesus experienced double marginality, Lee argues, when divine marginality intersected with the marginality imposed by human society. If followers of the Buddha and Jesus view their teachings as focused on marginality and those at the margins, our understanding of marginality will undoubtedly change. Marginality is not simply about being powerless or excluded; rather, it carries a deeper message and offers new guidance for the agency of those who find themselves at the margin for various reasons.

Religious traditions are not alone in understanding marginality as a power to rebound. Ueno Chizuko's definition of feminism helps us further enhance our new vision of marginality. Ueno states, "Feminism is from first to last an idea of, for and by, the minority. By minority, I mean those people who are oppressed, handicapped and/or discriminated against, and those who are weak and vulnerable. Feminism is not an idea that advocates that women should become powerful on a par with men, an idea I call a 'catching-up strategy,' but should be an idea that respects the dignity of minorities just as they are."[12]

To consider the position and value of the margin is not to swap the margin with the center, which would create another dichotomized structure of existence. Ueno's suggestion of respecting "the dignity of minorities just as they are" might sound like defeatist logic. But I would not interpret it that way. Physically, most women may not be on par with most men, but as Ueno states, "Why, simply because of this, should I [a woman] be forced to obey somebody else?"[13] Not all women's physical power is weaker than all men's. Differences in physical capacities and, in that sense, differences in various qualities of our existence should not be used to justify discriminatory actions or to subjugate one to the other. Ueno's assertion that feminism is not just about gender, but about the issues faced by everyone at the margin, and her emphasis that the margin's efforts to raise their voices should not mimic the practices of the center they challenge are lessons to which we must pay special attention in our discussion of marginality.

In a different context but using a similar logic, Black American Buddhist Lama Rod Owens tells us that challenging a racist society, in recognition of the suffering of Black Americans, should not be limited to actions that address the suffering of Black Americans alone. Instead, it means embracing all those who suffer injustice. According to Owens, "Political Blackness also embraces the lives of all people who survive systems of racial violence. My identity as being Black means I am always on the side of those of us who are targeted by systematic violence, including racism, queerphobia, transphobia, misogyny, ableism, and ageism," Owens declares. "A personal slogan of mine is that if you are marginalized, you are Black."[14]

When we consider all these cases together—that is, Buddhism's practice of humility through begging, Lee's interpretation of Jesus as a marginal figure, Ueno's call for feminism to apply to all minority groups, and Owens's call to identify all suffering marginalized groups as Black—we can easily use the concept of "solidarity" to characterize or label the topic. I have often advocated for the solidarity of the margin in this regard as well. My claim is that those at the margin should collaborate in challenging the power of the center, especially given the power imbalance between the center and the margin. Such activities have, in fact, been undertaken in recent history.

For example, in Washington, DC, in 2018, at the March for Our Lives—a student-led demonstration against assault weapons in response to school mass shootings—groups such as Code Pink: Women for Peace participated, showing their support for the students and their cause.

Similarly, at a vigil in Virginia organized by the Korean American community for the victims of the 2021 Atlanta spa shooting, in which the majority of the victims were Asian or Asian American women, African American groups also participated to show their solidarity.

The concept of minority solidarity is neither new nor merely theoretical; it has been a practice in our daily lives. I have frequently highlighted the significance of such solidarity, in action and in philosophical reflection. Yet some people have raised concerns about this call for solidarity—and rightly so. Those who are cautious or skeptical of its effectiveness reminded me of the collective memories of when solidarity was misused. In our recent history, solidarity has sometimes been harnessed to mobilize people for totalitarian purposes rather than to benefit those who responded to the call and acted in solidarity with others.

I believe that the ideas expressed by Ueno and Owens remain valid and that framing them as "the solidarity of the margin" aptly captures the essence of their contributions. I also invite Buddhist practitioners and Christians—although I am not a scholar of Christianity—to join in this spirit of solidarity, saying, "If you're at the margin, you're a Buddhist; if you're at the margin, you're a Christian." Unfortunately, the historical trajectories of these traditions make it challenging to accept such claims at face value. Nevertheless, I assert that the theoretical dimensions of Buddhism and marginality discussed in this book share a common vision for equality, freedom, and teachings we should strive for to realize these ideals.

But the potential totalitarian danger of solidarity cannot be ignored; it should also be actively examined. To that end, I invite the reader to consider what solidarity should entail if it aims to benefit each individual and is not exploited as a tool for a totalitarian regime. How should we characterize such practice of solidarity? To delve deeper into this issue, I introduce a Korean poet and his poetics of resistance.

Modern Korean poet Kim Suyŏng (1921–1968) once asserted that poetic freedom is synonymous with political freedom. For him, an individual's freedom to express themselves in poetry without being constrained by the social system or literary conventions, such as poetic diction, is equivalent to political freedom. Kim argues that liberated utterance is possible only when we are free to be creative socially, politically, and linguistically. His poetry vividly illustrates how he practiced this vision. He was unafraid to use unconventional, "nonpoetic" references, such as "diarrhea" or "bathroom tissues," in poems that criticize the political situation of South Korea during his time. In several of his poems, he also reflects on how social change might occur and the forms in which individuals should engage with it.

In "Blue Sky," he writes,

> Those who have ever soared
> for the sake of freedom
> know . . .
> why freedom is blended with the smell of blood,
> why revolution
> is lonely,
> why revolution
> has to be lonely.[15]

Written in the aftermath of the April Revolution in 1960, when the South Korean people took to the streets to demand the resignation of President Seungman Rhee, the poem reflects Kim's perspective on the nature of freedom and revolution. Although revolution can be sparked by the collective solidarity of those who march and act together, this solidarity does not and cannot ensure a complete sense of belonging.

On the contrary, Kim asserts that revolution is lonely work. During massive protests—such as the April 19 Revolution in South Korea or, more recently, the Women's March or March for Our Lives in the United States—people chant slogans and march together, fostering a sense of belonging among participants who share physical or, in modern times, virtual space. Surrounded by numerous people working toward what appears to be the same cause, participants often experience a strong sense of belonging. This sense of community reflects the commitment of individuals to the cause of their activism. But such surface-level solidarity does not necessarily mean that every member shares the same goal. Despite the apparent unity fueled by the energy of the large crowd, there is neither a guarantee that each individual participant is envisioning the same goal nor a promise that the collective commitment will lead to visible results. The uncertainty regarding the nature of the participants and the outcome of the activism is often overlooked as those involved in a revolution or protest cheer for the goal to be achieved. In contrast to this common phenomenon, Kim directs our attention to the loneliness that inevitably arises when confronting the uncertain future and the potential diversity of participants' vision of the end results.

The loneliness of revolution that Kim so explicitly expresses in his poem defines what I call reflexive solidarity (as opposed to totalitarian solidarity) or reflexive engagement (as opposed to conformist engagement). In totalitarian solidarity, both those who call for solidarity and those who respond are certain that their goal is achievable and that their cause is clear and just. Reflexive solidarity, or reflexive engagement, on the other hand, arises from a belief in the power of possibility and the necessity of action. But necessity and possibility do not have a certain outcome; one participates despite doubts about both.

Because an individual has only the possibility of success, not a guaranteed outcome, and yet is convinced that action is inevitable, they are continually compelled to reflect on their actions and the movement's direction. The loneliness of revolution, in this sense, is essential for any revolution to have meaning and an authentic impact, whether said revolution is social, political, individual, or mental. This can be likened to religious practice, where faith is required but doubt must also be part of that faith if it is not to be a blind adherence to doctrines.

My students often say that Buddhism is an individualistic religion. Even after learning that Buddhism understands existence through relational identity and teaches that no being has a permanent, independent essence, their view rarely changes. One primary reason for this is that Buddhism requires cultivation, a process that each individual must undertake on their own and that no one else can do it for them. The image of Zen masters meditating alone in the mountains, seemingly detached from the events of the secular world, has likely contributed to my students' perception of Buddhist individualism. But when my students claim that Buddhism is individualistic, they are confusing two distinct types of individualism.

Kim Iryŏp, a modern Korean Buddhist nun and thinker I introduced in chapter 1, makes a distinction between old individualism and new individualism. She describes old individualism, which she also refers to as bourgeois individualism, as being rooted in a group consciousness that "stirs up all the impure instincts in us."[16] This is the type of individualism that serves the interests of a privileged group and is maintained through the individual's conformity to that group. In contrast, the new individualism she supports is marked by a person's continuous effort to self-examine and discover an authentic self with true agency. This form of individualism is defined by a being's full awareness of their true self and their efforts to uncover it without being controlled by external forces or constraints. Iryŏp's concept of old individualism helps us recognize the illusions behind the notions of "individual" and "individualism," which have become buzzwords in our modern world.

Individualism is often defined as supporting the individual's autonomy, freedom, and rights. But when we reflect on our lives in modern society, it becomes evident that many aspects of our existence are increasingly shaped by socially constructed frameworks—such as education, which focuses on the accumulation of information; the financial market, centered on wealth accumulation; the drive to expand one's ego; social media; streaming services; and more. How free are we, really? How autonomous are our decisions? Iryŏp's concept of new individualism urges us to recognize the fallacy of autonomy as a misleading promise of modernist individualism and truly take ownership of ourselves. But what does it mean to have self-ownership when people are marginalized in society because of factors like gender, race, ethnicity, or economic status? Can those at the margins still strive for authentic selves despite the structural violence they face? Can they participate in their society's knowledge production?

Kim Suyŏng addresses this issue in "Grass," his last poem before his untimely death in an automobile accident at age forty-seven:

Grass lies down.
Blown by the east wind
that drives rain,
it lay down
and wept at last.
It wept more because of cloudiness,
then lay down again.

Grass lies down.
It lies down more quickly than the wind.
It weeps more quickly than the wind,
and it rises before the wind.

It gets cloudy, and grass lies down.
To its ankle,
to its sole, it lies down.
Lying down after the wind,
it rises before the wind.
Weeping later than the wind,
it laughs before the wind.
It gets cloudy, and the root lies down.[17]

There is a deconstructive movement underlying Kim's depiction of the resilience and resistance of grass. At first, the grass appears weak, a victim of the forces that exert power over it. It acknowledges its underprivileged position, its lack of power, yet it does not surrender. In response to the power that seeks to control it, the grass creates its own movement, navigating the flow of the wind. By the end, the grass lies down, pushed by the wind, but rises again before the wind, asserting its agency despite the forces against it. It weeps, but it also laughs, because it has created its own pattern. The wind's power tries to shake the grass, but it cannot break it, as the grass moves through its own rhythm to navigate the wind's force. The grass confronts the wind on its own terms, meaning that it can weep and laugh while facing the wind, the external constraints of the structured system, in its own way. Through this self-directed movement, the grass maintains its resilience, turning apparent vulnerability into strength as it responds to the forces that seek to control it.

The Japanese philosopher Tanabe Hajime (1885–1962) once said that freedom means "turning contingency into the choice and decision of the subject." He argued that freedom involves "transforming 'having no principle' into 'having its own principle.' "[18] In this view, freedom is not merely the absence of constraints, but the active process of shaping our own principles and decisions in response to the contingencies of life.

Freedom is not premade; it is something we must earn at great cost. Kim even more radically describes it in "Blue Sky" as "blended with the smell of blood." But earning freedom also means creatively responding to whatever happens in our lives, as exemplified by the movements of grass in "Grass." The grass's ability to engage with the wind and create its own rhythm symbolizes the active and creative engagement necessary to shape our freedom, even amidst external forces far stronger than ourselves.

At the heart of this activity lies taking responsibility as the agent of our own actions. Life is made up of a series of contingencies, and a full understanding of their structure and rationale often escapes us. We are typically left with only partial information. The contingency of life's events is not confined to those in disadvantaged positions. Even those at the center, often perceived as powerful, are subject to life's unpredictability, despite their belief in their invincibility. The illusion of control does not protect anyone from the uncertainties of existence. When the Buddha claimed that his teaching was aimed at eliminating suffering, the twist was in the implication that Buddhism is not only for those at the designated margins; rather, this asserts that everyone is marginalized in some way. No one is immune to aging, sickness, and eventual death, let alone the various other struggles that life throws our way. In this sense, everyone is at the margin, experiencing the insecurity that arises from the contingency of life.

The act of "transforming the contingency" into choice and thus creating our own pattern for life out of no predetermined design is closely related to the Buddhist concepts of karma and cultivation. As I briefly mentioned in chapter 1, karma, one of the most well-known elements of Buddhism in the West, literally means "action," which encompasses physical, mental, and verbal actions. What is crucial in Buddhist karma is intention. Each of us is brought into this world, and, as existentialism often points out, we are thrown into a world of contingency. Rational explanations of life and life events quickly encounter limitations and even dead ends when attempting to explain why the world is dominated by inequality, discrimination, poverty, and the unfair distribution of wealth or why particular events unfold in an individual's life. In Kim's poem, the grass didn't choose to be grass, and the wind didn't choose to be wind, even though the power dynamic between them reflects a hierarchical relationship. The difference arises when the grass decides to transform the contingent reality of being driven and swayed by the wind into freedom by creating its own pattern.

Karma, in essence, is about making choices. Each moment, we can decide on everything from what to eat for dinner to what career path to take and what values to prioritize in life. But how do we determine if we're making the right or most beneficial choice? Buddhism suggests that cultivating the mind is not just helpful but actually essential to making better decisions. Buddhism asserts that cultivation aids us in making choices that lead to positive outcomes, with the key difference being that it helps us focus on how the action relates to suffering. The goal is to minimize suffering and promote wisdom, compassion, and understanding through thoughtful decision-making.

When an action is likely to cause suffering for us or for others, it is not recommended; conversely, when an action is likely to alleviate suffering, both for ourselves and others, it is encouraged. The reflexive solidarity or engagement I have proposed requires us to learn how to transform contingency into freedom, a process that is deepened through inner cultivation. Much like the loneliness of revolution, orienting and reorienting our perspectives is inherently lonely work, as it demands a commitment that cannot be carried out by proxy. It is a personal, ongoing effort to shape our understanding and actions in the world.

The inner transformation essential to this reflexive engagement extends beyond an individual's personal life; it forms the foundation of social change. Rima Vesely-Flad, a professor of philosophy and religious studies, connects Black Buddhism with Black radical philosophies that challenge and combat racism and discrimination. She observes, "Buddhist teachings and practices liberate Black people from psychological suffering."[19] Characterizing Black Buddhism as encompassing both meditation and the rituals of Buddhism, she writes, "The socially vilified Black body is, for the Black Buddhist, a profound and reclaimed vehicle for liberation."[20] Vesely-Flad's definition of the dual positioning of Black bodies as both socially disparaged and a source of liberation is insightful for considering the concept of marginality.

By approaching marginality with a creative mindset, we can recognize the embodied form of marginality as it manifests in various ways, as I have discussed in this book: gender, race, ethnicity, economic status, and many more. Marginality exists in relation to the center, and, like the push and pull of grass and wind in Kim's poem, the margin's desire for freedom and the practice of turning contingency into freedom provide agency for the margin in understanding its own position and engaging with the center. Marginality becomes the source of the margin's liberation. Reflexive engagement with the margin opens the possibility of transforming that marginality into a source of freedom.

Cho Seihŭi, the author of *A Dwarf Launches a Little Ball*, gave an interview in 2005 marking the two-hundredth reprint of his novel, nearly thirty years after its first publication. Instead of expressing joy at the book's popularity, he voiced despair over the fact that the younger generation today still feels that the issues addressed in his novel are relevant. He had hoped that they would see the story of the factory workers, the discrimination against marginalized people, and the extreme polarization of wealth as issues of the past. Many people would share this despair. The world seems even more polarized today than when Cho expressed his concern over the relevance of his 1978 novel to young South Koreans in 2005. The despair deepens each time we read about the unequal distribution of wealth, global poverty, racial conflict, hate crimes, gun violence, and all of the other challenges we face in our time. But our despair should not lead us to inaction or pessimism.

Marginality inevitably creates insecurity, but it is also the space through which we must leap to challenge the structures that assign people to the margins. Changes may take time, but even the smallest shifts can occur as those at the margins act, and their cumulative effect will propel society forward. The margin is not only a space that the marginalized must endure while confronting the power of the center. Historically, it has also been a space where new and creative ideas emerge, often challenging the stagnation of the center and claiming their own value. Thus, the margin reconfigures the center and what the center represents, since the margin is the force for social change.

Epilogue

Marginality is closely related to the principles and practices commonly referred to in recent years as DEI—diversity, equity, and inclusion. In this book, I argue that the implementation of DEI has often failed to fully realize its potential, highlighting issues such as tokenism and insufficient engagement with systemic inequities, including disparities in cultural capital. The social and political landscape in the United States shifted drastically with the start of the second Trump administration in January 2025, as I completed this book. Within two days of taking office, President Trump issued executive orders to eliminate DEI initiatives across federal agencies.[1] Federal government websites quickly purged DEI-related content.[2] DEI practices were even cited as a contributing factor in a tragic aviation disaster that claimed sixty-seven lives.[3]

DEI initiatives emerged to address structural inequities in American society by expanding opportunities for historically marginalized groups. Several events amplified DEI's importance: the 2020 pandemic exposed healthcare disparities, while the #MeToo and Black Lives Matter movements revealed persistent gender and racial discrimination. Business research, such as McKinsey's diversity studies, demonstrated that workplace diversity enhances organizational performance and innovation. Their reports documented the benefits of inclusion in business while showing ongoing challenges in achieving equitable representation.[4] McKinsey's 2023 State of Diversity report revealed three key findings: companies with diverse workforces achieved better financial performance, overall workforce diversity increased since previous studies, but leadership positions still lack fair representation, particularly for women and racial/ethnic minorities at senior levels.[5]

Opposition to DEI has also been vocal. Some critics view DEI initiatives as discriminatory against white people and men. Following the Supreme Court's 2023 decision to strike down affirmative action in college admissions, many companies have scaled back or eliminated their DEI programs. This trend has accelerated under the second Trump administration, with companies like Google, Amazon, Meta, Ford, McDonald's, and Target making such changes.

The trend has raised concerns among DEI supporters,[6] while DEI opponents tell a different story. In place of diversity, equity, inclusion, critics now advocate for MEI (merit, excellence, and intelligence). Ironically, this promotion of MEI assumes DEI does not value merit, excellence, and intelligence. On the contrary, DEI advocates argue that people with merit, excellence, and intelligence have been excluded from fair evaluation based on these qualities as a result of structural discrimination against certain groups based on gender, ethnicity, social class, and other group identities. Martin Luther King Jr.'s famous "I Have a Dream" speech addresses exactly this point when he said, "I have a dream that my four little children will one day live in a nation where they will not be judged by the color of their skin but by the content of their character." Critics of DEI argue that since "character" or merit is the measure of an individual's value, skin color—or identity—should not be part of evaluation.

Another irony emerges here: for people of color to be judged not by their skin color, or women not by their reproductive organ, but by "the content of their character," skin color or gender must still be considered because of centuries-old racism or millennia-old patriarchal structures. In today's highly polarized world, where major issues including DEI face sharply divided views, governments' policies at both federal and state levels that systematically eliminate programs such as DEI leave underprivileged people without resources to challenge existing inequalities and structural injustice. What tools remain for marginalized groups? How can they continue to challenge inequities that undermine their dignity and humanity when society reinstates deeply rooted discrimination while accusing them of being swindlers who purportedly abuse the idea of justice to mask their alleged incompetence?

Over the coming years—and already—many people will grapple with these questions, seeking venues to challenge and protest discrimination and oppression of marginalized groups. The current situation teaches us that the path to a more diverse, equitable, and inclusive society cannot rely on a single concept or policy, and it need not be labeled solely as DEI. While policies are necessary for an idea to effectively impact a large number of people and organizations, these policies can be distorted by users or eliminated by those in power, as we are witnessing today.

Like the grass in Kim Suyŏng's poem that navigates the power of the wind, marginalized communities must learn what such navigation requires. Like the dwarf who launched a paper plane from atop a chimney and the math teacher who teaches freedom and hope, these communities need to discover diverse ways to express, affirm, and sustain their hope and freedom—and to act accordingly. In this process, we must understand that "the margin" does not represent a fixed group; our identities are always complex results of intersectionality. The value of education in the United States offers one example of this complexity.

Earlier, I addressed how equal opportunity practices in US higher education have fallen short of helping students from underrepresented groups, who lack cultural capital as much as financial resources. Yet in a different context, such a diagnosis might appear to be privileged discourse. According to the US Census Bureau's Educational Attainment data from 2022, only 37.7 percent of people in the United States aged twenty-five or older have a bachelor's degree or higher.[7] Education, like anything else, can be a matter of individual choice, and getting a college degree need not be part of everyone's life plan. But according to the US Bureau of Labor Statistics, more education correlates with higher income and lower unemployment rates.

The May 2023 report of the US Bureau of Labor Statistics states, "Workers age twenty-five and over without a high school diploma had median weekly earnings of $682. Workers whose highest level of education was a diploma made $853 per week, or just over 25 percent more than those who didn't finish high school—and earnings improved with every level of education completed."[8] In 2022, those without a diploma faced a 5.5 percent unemployment rate, the highest among comparison groups, with "unemployment rates decreasing as education increased."[9] While individual outcomes vary depending on the field of expertise and personal circumstances, these statistics confirm that education represents a significant privilege in our society. This insight should not be used to silence those who feel marginalized in higher education but rather help us recognize the complex relationship between margin and center and understand how privilege takes on different meanings when viewed from various perspectives.

Neither the margin nor the center is fixed. This understanding lies at the heart of minority solidarity and reflexive engagement. Minority solidarity does not simply mean that fixed minority groups should collaborate to challenge an immutable center. A person might occupy a minority position as an Asian woman in a patriarchal, West-centered society while simultaneously holding privilege as an educated intellectual in a capitalist, education-revering society. Similarly, a person might experience marginalization as a queer woman in a patriarchal, homophobic society while still benefiting from white privilege in a white-centered world.

Developing and cultivating the capacity to recognize the multidimensional reality of our existence—and the diverse identities we carry throughout life—remains our central challenge. Through awakening to our multidimensional and intersectional identities, we may foster care and understanding for others, which becomes a force that challenges the center's rigid and often authoritarian categorization of people. This force can form the foundation for broader movements of protest and resistance that demands social change.

The political philosopher José Medina emphasizes the epistemic and communicative power of protests, particularly under conditions of oppression. Epistemology in philosophy concerns knowledge acquisition—how we come to know and understand. By emphasizing the epistemic nature of protest, Medina asserts that protests, especially those by marginalized people under oppression, are not mere instruments for conveying messages but spaces for *"transformative learning."*[10] He challenges the idea that protesters arrive with "prepackaged communicative contents" to inform society.[11] Instead, he argues that protesters learn about their causes while participating in protest, and through this process, they discover more about their own positions and the agenda their protest supports.

Medina's discussion of protest as a learning process aligns with Kim Suyŏng's conception that revolution is solitary work, which I discussed earlier. Amid the multitude of protesters, we learn about ourselves as much as the goals the protest advances. Medina emphasizes that protest is not only a form of physical activism but also an epistemic act. Various religious traditions have, for millennia, explored the concept and practice of resistance within the mental and epistemic realms. Cultivation in Buddhism, particularly Zen (Chan/Sŏn) Buddhism trains practitioners on a path toward radical mental transformation, known as awakening or enlightenment. This mental transformation in Buddhism extends beyond our thinking process; thought itself is an action in Buddhism and must lead to physical action. We cannot simply understand that our existence is connected with others while continuing to exercise self-centered egoistic actions. A modern Korean Sǒn master once said that feeding a hungry dog is a more authentic form of practicing Buddhism than making offerings to the Buddha at a temple.

Understanding mental revolution as a form of action reveals the deeper and broader significance of self-reflection, not just as an individual practice, but as the starting point for collective resistance. Mental transformation occurs within individuals—which some might dismiss as a weak form of resistance due to its seemingly limited scope—yet history shows how an individual's mental power can spread to millions. Buddhism teaches that each person can catalyze such change through their own transformation, compelling them to engage with others to improve life for all. This mental revolution demands self-reflection—not a sign of weakness, but rather a demonstration of strength in examining oneself and an individual's values during times of difficulty and apparent hopelessness. Reflexive engagement emphasized in Buddhism, combined with the epistemic transformation Medina describes in protest participants, can generate a collective force capable of reconfiguring the power of the center that wield their authority as if there were no tomorrow. Reflexive solidarity offers a path forward even when the force of the center feels overwhelming. Through this process of transformation, those at the margins continue to reclaim their values and agency. Reflexive engagement, in this sense, should encompass both mental and physical actions that foster individual and social transformation. This very capacity to act—to resist—marks the beginning of hope.

Notes

Introduction

1. Pak Ch'iu, *Sasang kwa hyŏnsil* (*Ideas and reality*), ed. Yun Taesŏk and Yun Miran (Seoul: Inha taehakkyo ch'ulp'anbu, 2010), 15. Translation mine.

1. Departure

1. Julia Kristeva, *Étrangers à nous-memes* (Paris: Gallimard, 1988), 9; English translation, *Strangers to Ourselves*, trans. Leon S. Roudiez (New York: Columbia University Press, 1991), 2.
2. Kristeva, *Étrangers à nous-memes*, 34; *Strangers to Ourselves*, 21.
3. Ralph Ellison, *Invisible Man* (New York: Vintage, 1972), 3.
4. Jean-Paul Sartre, *Existentialism Is a Humanism* (New Haven, CT: Yale University Press, 2007), 22.
5. Sartre, *Existentialism Is a Humanism*, 22.
6. Søren Kierkegaard, *Fear and Trembling and Repetition*, ed. and trans. Howard V. Hong and Edna H. Hong (Princeton, NJ: Princeton University Press, 1983), 55–81.
7. Thich Nhat Hanh, *The Heart of Understanding: Commentaries on the Prajnaparamita Heart Sūtra* (Berkeley, CA: Parallax Press, 2009), 3.

1. DEPARTURE

8. Jean-Paul Sartre, *Nausea*, trans. Lloyd Alexander (New York: New Directions, 1964), 147.

9. Hannah Arendt, *Eichmann in Jerusalem: A Report on the Banality of Evil* (New York: Penguin, 1963), 35.

10. Arendt, *Eichmann in Jerusalem*, 35.

11. Kim Iryŏp, *Ŏnŭ sudoin ŭi hoesang* (Yesan, South Korea: Sudŏksa, 1960), 1; English translation, *Reflections of a Zen Buddhist Nun: Essays by Zen Master Kim Iryŏp*, trans. Jin Y. Park (Honolulu: University of Hawai'i Press, 2014), 29.

12. Joseph H. Carens, *The Ethics of Immigration* (New York: Oxford University Press, 2013), 192.

13. Kristeva, *Étrangers à nous-memes*, 46; *Strangers to Ourselves*, 29.

14. Benedict Anderson, *Imagined Communities: Reflections on the Origin and Spread of Nationalism* (London: Verso, 1983), 145. Rejecting the common assumption that a nation-state must have existed before the emergence of nationalism, Anderson argues that nationalism was necessary for the newly emerged power group to legitimize its authority and, in doing so, create a nation-state. He says, "nationalism has to be understood by aligning it, not with self-consciously held political ideologies, but with the large cultural systems that preceded it, out of which as well as against which—it came into being" (12). Nationalism assumes a certain form of homogeneous agreement among a group regarding the values of its community. Anderson argues that this understanding was not created by a nation-state but through various cultural changes at the time, such as the emergence of newspapers, which fostered a sense of community through shared temporality. Importantly, the fact that the nation-state is an imagined community does not make it any less real, Anderson emphasizes (227). A core question, then, is whether nationalism is used or can be used for the benefit of its members, or if it is only employed to promote the ideology of those in power. Anderson refers to the latter as "official nationalism," explaining: "Official nationalism was from the start a conscious, self-protective policy, intimately linked to the preservation of imperial-dynastic interests. . . . The one persistent feature of this style of nationalism was, and is, that it is official—i.e., something emanating from the state, and serving the interests of the state first and foremost" (159). It is not difficult to draw a connection between official

nationalism and state violence, as it often involves the excessive use of state power.

15. Anderson, *Imagined Communities*, 6–7.

16. Brunno Kato and Yoshiro Tamur, trans., *The Threefold Lotus Sūtra* (London: Kosei Publishing Company, 1989), 135. Translation modified. The portrayal of women in the Lotus Sutra has indeed sparked significant scholarly debate. One of the central issues is whether the text demonstrates that women can attain enlightenment, thereby supporting gender justice within Buddhism. Lucinda Joy Peach, for example, emphasizes the multidimensional nature of women's position in Buddhism as revealed in the Lotus Sutra. An important issue to note, Peach argues, is that "the influence of images does not necessarily correlate in any direct way to the actual status of women in a particular social location." See Lucinda Joy Peach, "Social Responsibility, Sex Change, and Salvation: Gender Justice in the *Lotus Sūtra*," *Philosophy East and West* 52, no. 1 (January 2002): 50–51. This is a poignant insight, as even though contemporary scholars interpret body transformation literature, including the Lotus Sutra and the Vimalakīrti Sutra, in the context of women's position in Buddhism, there is no definitive evidence that these scriptures were originally understood to promote women's status within the tradition.

17. In his *Philosophy of History*, Hegel wrote: "The History of the World travels from East to West, for Europe is absolutely the end of History, Asia the beginning. The History of the World has an East . . . for although the Earth forms a sphere, History performs no circle around it, but has on the contrary a determinate East, viz., Asia. Here rises the outward physical Sun, and in the West it sinks down: here consentaneously rises the Sun of self-consciousness, which diffuses nobler brilliance." G. W. F. Hegel, *The Philosophy of History*, trans. J. Sibree (Buffalo, NY: Prometheus Books, 1991), 103.

18. Edmund Husserl, "Philosophy and the Crisis of European Humanity," *The Crisis of European Sciences and Transcendental Phenomenology: An Introduction to Phenomenological Philosophy*, trans. David Carr (Evanston, IL: Northwestern University Press, 1970), 280.

19. See discussions on this topic in Wilhelm Halbfass, *India and Europe* (Albany: State University of New York Press, 1988), 437.

1. DEPARTURE

20. Kwok-ying Lau, *Phenomenology and Intercultural Philosophy: Toward a New Cultural Flesh* (Berlin: Springer, 2016), 56.

21. Bryan W. Van Norden, "Chinese Philosophy Is Missing from U.S. Philosophy Departments. Should We Care?" *The Conversation*, May 18, 2016, https://theconversation.com/chinese-philosophy-is-missing-from -u-s-philosophy-departments-should-we-care-56550. Also see Jay L. Garfield and Bryan W. Van Norden, "If Philosophy Won't Diversify, Let's Call It What It Really Is," *New York Times*, May 11, 2016, https:// www.nytimes.com/2016/05/11/opinion/if-philosophy-wont-diversify -lets-call-it-what-it-really-is.html.

22. Hannah Arendt, *On Violence* (New York: Harcourt, 1970), 44.

23. "A Conversation with James Baldwin," American Archive of Public Broadcasting, https://americanarchive.org/catalog?q=The+Negro+and +the+American+Promise%3A+James+Baldwin&utf8=%E2%9C%93 &f[access_types][]=online.

24. James Baldwin, *I Am Not Your Negro*, comp. and ed. Raoul Peck (New York: Vintage International, 2016), 108–09.

2. Exclusion

1. Eric Schwitzgebel, "Citation of Women and Ethnic Minorities in the Stanford Encyclopedia of Philosophy," *The Splintered Mind*, August 7, 2014, http://schwitzsplinters.blogspot.com/2014/08/citation-of-women -and-ethnic-minorities.html.

2. Donald Kagan, "Western Values are Central," *New York Times*, May 4, 1991.

3. Henry Louis Gates Jr., "Whose Culture Is It, Anyway?" *New York Times*, May 4, 1991.

4. Frederick Douglass, *Narrative of the Life of Frederic Douglass and the Fourth of July Speech* (Orinda: SeaWolf Press, 2020), 111.

5. Douglass, *Narrative of the Life of Frederic Douglass*, 112. Italics original.

6. Yussi puin, *Choch'immun* (Seoul: Shinwŏnmunhwasa, 2004), 17. Translation mine.

7. See Jon Marcus, "America's Next Union Battlefield May Be on Campus," *Washington Post*, March 25, 2022, https://www.washingtonpost .com/education/2022/03/25/colleges-faculty-unions-labor/.

8. William A. Herbert, Jacob Apkarian, and Joseph van der Naald, "2020 Supplementary Directory of New Bargaining Agents and Contracts in Institutions of Higher Education, 2013–2019," National Center for the Study of Collective Bargaining in Higher Education and the Professions (November 2020), 13. https://webedit2.hunter.cuny.edu /ncscbhep/assets/files/SupplementalDirectory-2020-FINAL.pdf.

The National Education Association (NEA) ran an article on the phenomenon: Mary Ellen Flannery, "'We Stepped Up and Fought Back': Behind the Explosive Growth of New Faculty Unions," *neaToday*, November 29, 2020.

9. "Where Are the Priorities?: The Annual Report of the Economic Status of the Professions, 2007–08," March–April 2008, 16. American Association of University Professors, https://www.aaup.org/sites /default/files/Mar-Apr2008_Feature_0.pdf. For the past two decades, the situation has not improved. For example, according to the "IPEDS Academic Workforce, Fall 2002 to 2023" survey, the number of full-time tenure-track faculty in 2002 was 110,856, while tenured faculty numbered 256,923. In 2023, these numbers were 102,815 and 272,603, respectively. This shows little change in tenure-track and tenured faculty numbers over twenty years. In fact, the data shows that new tenure-track positions declined during this period. In contrast, part-time faculty numbers grew from 476,462 in 2002 to 573,500 in 2023, representing an increase of over 20 percent, https:// data.aaup.org/academic-workforce/.

10. "How Much Are Public-College Presidents Paid?" *Chronicle of Higher Education*, August 17, 2022, https://www.chronicle.com/article/president -pay-public-colleges/. "How Much Are Private-College Presidents Paid?" *Chronicle of Higher Education*, August 17, 2022, https://www.chronicle .com/article/president-pay-private-colleges.

11. American Association of University Professors, "The Annual Report on the Economic Status of the Profession, 2022–2023," https://www .aaup.org/file/ARES-2022-23.pdf, 7.

12. Benjamin Ginsberg, *The Fall of the Faculty: The Rise of the All-Administrative University and Why It Matters* (New York: Oxford University Press, 2011), 3.

13. Paul Tough, "Americans Are Losing Faith in the Value of College: Whose Fault is That?" *New York Times Magazine*, September 5, 2023.

14. Pierre Bourdieu, "Cultural Reproduction and Social Reproduction," in *Knowledge, Education, and Cultural Change: Papers in the Sociology of Education*, ed. Richard Brown, British Sociological Association (London: Routledge, 1973), 71–112.

15. This situation has changed radically in government and business in the second Trump administration. Within forty-eight hours of taking office, President Trump moved to eliminate DEI throughout the federal government, and companies have scaled down or eliminated their DEI programs. I discuss this development in the epilogue.

16. Cho Se-Hui, *Nanjangi ka ssoaollin chakŭn kong* (Seoul: Munhak kwa chisŏngsa, 1978), 116; English translation, *A Dwarf Launches a Little Ball*, trans. Chun Kyung-Ja (Seoul: Jimoondang Publishing Company, 2002), 42.

17. Cho, *Nanjangi ka ssoaollin chakŭn kong*, 91-92; English translation, Cho, *A Dwarf Launches a Little Ball*, 16–17. Translation modified.

18. Jacques Derrida, *La Carte postale: de Socrate à Freud et au-delà* (Paris: Flammarion, 1980), 97; English translation, *The Post Card: From Socrates to Freud and Beyond*, trans. Alan Bass (Chicago: University of Chicago Press, 1987), 87.

19. Jacques Derrida, "I Have a Taste for the Secret," in Jacques Derrida and Maurizio Ferraris, *A Taste for the Secret*, trans. Giacomo Donis, ed. Giacomo Donis and David Webb (Cambridge: Polity, 2001), 38.

3. Violence

1. Jeffrey Reiman and Paul Leighton, *The Rich Get Richer and the Poor Get Prison: Thinking Critically About Class and Criminal Justice*, 13th ed. (New York: Routledge, 2023), 80. Italics in the original.

2. Reiman and Leighton, *The Rich Get Richer and the Poor Get Prison*, xiv.

3. Reiman and Leighton, *The Rich Get Richer and the Poor Get Prison*, 5. Italics in the original.

4. Reiman and Leighton, *The Rich Get Richer and the Poor Get Prison*, xiii. Italics in the original.

5. Han Kang, *Ch'aesik chuŭija* (Seoul: Ch'angbi, 2007), 9; English translation, *The Vegetarian*, trans. Deborah Smith (New York: Hogarth, 2017), 11.

6. Han, *Ch'aesik chuŭija*, 142–143; English translation, Han, *The Vegetarian*, 122.

7. Gi-Wook Shin and Kyung Moon Hwang, eds., *Contentious Kwangju: The May 18 Uprising in Korea's Past and Present* (Lanham, MD: Rowman & Littlefield, 2003), xv.

8. Gwangju and Kwangju refer to the same city. The difference in spelling arises from the use of different romanization systems for the Korean language. The former follows the Revised Romanization of Korean, while the latter uses the McCune-Reischauer system.

9. Shin and Hwang, *Contentious Kwangju*, xvi.

10. Shin and Hwang, *Contentious Kwangju*, 44–45.

11. Shin and Hwang, *Contentious Kwangju*, xvii.

12. One of the most popular early TV dramatizations of the Gwangju incident was *Moraeshigye* (*Hourglass*), which aired in 1995 and achieved an average viewing rate of 46 percent. Since then, the Gwangju Uprising has been depicted in various films, literary works, TV series, and songs. The extremely high viewing rate of *Hourglass* not only reflects the success of the series but also highlights how the Korean people had been largely cut off from information about the incident, thus preventing the creation of a public space in which to reflect upon it.

Don Baker warns readers that any depiction of Gwangju risks oversimplifying the situation (see Don Baker, "Victims and Heroes: Competing Visions of May 18" in Shin and Hwang, eds., *Contentious Kwangju*). While there were those who fought against the military dictatorship and for democracy, there were also individuals who, although not driven by such ideals, were forced to join the protest simply because of the circumstances. One cannot judge participation of the former as authentic and participation of the latter as inauthentic without considering their context. As Baker states, "We thus have competing 'myths' of May 18. Whichever interpretation of May 18 we adopt, we run the risk of simplifying, and therefore distorting, the full complexity of the events in Kwangju two decades ago" (104). Positionality and perspective are inevitably at play when interpreting a historical event or even a personal experience, which highlights the danger of centralized or official interpretations. In official history, the lives of marginalized groups are often flattened and compromised to serve the ideology of the center.

159

13. Walter Benjamin, "Critique of Violence," in *Reflections: Essays, Aphorisms, Autobiographical Writings*, trans. Edmund Jephcott (New York: Mariner Books, 2019), 312.

14. Han Kang, *Sonyŏn i onda* (Seoul: Ch'angbi, 2014), 17; English translation, *Human Acts*, trans. Deborah Smith (New York: Hogarth, 2016), 17.

15. Han, *Sonyŏn i onda*, 182; *Human Acts*, 172. Translation mine.

16. Chizuko Ueno, *Nationalism and Gender*, trans. Beverley Yamamoto (Melbourne: Trans Pacific Press, 2006), 65.

17. Ueno, *Nationalism and Gender*, 146.

18. Ueno, *Nationalism and Gender*, 45.

19. Ueno, *Nationalism and Gender*, 48.

20. Miranda Fricker, *Epistemic Injustice: Power and the Ethics of Knowing* (New York: Oxford University Press, 2007), 17.

21. Ueno, *Nationalism and Gender*, 144.

22. Toni Morrison, "Black Studies Center Public Dialogue, Part 2" (lecture, Portland State University, Portland, Oregon, May 30, 1975), https://soundcloud.com/portland-state-library/portland-state-black-studies-1?mc_cid=7a27cfd978&mc_eid=e2efbcffa9.

23. Jacques Derrida, "I Have a Taste for the Secret," in Jacques Derrida and Maurizio Ferraris, *A Taste for the Secret*, trans. Giacomo Donis, ed. Giacomo Donis and David Webb (Polity, 2001), 41.

4. Minority Against Minority

1. Shelley Sang-Hee Lee, *Koreatown, Los Angeles: Immigration, Race, and the "American Dream"* (Stanford, CA: Stanford University Press, 2022), 39.

2. Shelley Sang-Hee Lee, *Koreatown, Los Angeles*, 27.

3. William Overend, "Koreans Pursue the American Dream . . . and Find Land of Opportunity," *Los Angeles Times*, September 10, 1978.

4. Chang-rae Lee, *Native Speaker* (New York: Riverhead Books, 1995), 6.

5. Chang-rae Lee, *Native Speaker*, 45.

6. Chang-rae Lee, *Native Speaker*, 45.

7. Chang-rae Lee, *Native Speaker*, 309.

4. MINORITY AGAINST MINORITY

8.   Nancy Abelmann and John Lie, *Blue Dreams: Korean Americans and the Los Angeles Riots* (Cambridge, MA: Harvard University Press, 1995), 161.

9.   Ellen D. Wu, *The Color of Success: Asian Americans and the Origins of the Model Minority* (Princeton, NJ: Princeton University Press, 2014), 2. Italics in the original.

10. Wu, *The Color of Success*, 2. Italics in original.

11. Nishida Kitaro (1870–1945) is credited as the founder of the Kyoto School, a modern Japanese philosophical school associated with Kyoto University. Nishida introduced the concept of "absolute contradictory self-identity" in several of his works, including his 1938 article "Human Being." See Nishida Kitaro, "Human Being," in *Ontology of Production: Three Essays*, trans. William Haver (Durham, NC: Duke University Press, 2012), 144–185.

12. Chang-rae Lee, *Native Speaker*, 49.

13. Christine Choy, *Rodney King: Koreatown Reacts* (Film News Now Foundation, 2016), 00:00:55. Choy also directed the 1987 film *Who Killed Vincent Chin?*

14. Chang-rae Lee, *Native Speaker*, 300.

15. Confucius, *The Analects*, 17.25. Translation mine.

16. Chenyang Li, "The Confucian Concept of Jen and the Feminist Ethics of Care: A Comparative Study," in *The Sage and the Second Sex: Confucianism, Ethics, and Gender*, ed. Chenyang Li (Chicago: Open Court, 2000), 35.

17. Mengzi, *Book of Mengzi*, Book III, B2; English translation, *A Source Book in Chinese Philosophy*, trans. Wing-Tsit Chan (Princeton, NJ: Princeton University Press, 1963), 72.

18. See JaHyun Kim Haboush, "The Confucianization of Korean Society," in *East Asian Religion: Confucian Heritage and its Modern Adaptation*, ed. Gilbert Rozman (Princeton, NJ: Princeton University Press, 1991), 84. According to Haboush, before Korean society underwent full Confucianization in the late seventeenth century and solidified its patriarchal, patrilocal, and patrilineal social system, women's positions were much more flexible. The responsibility for hosting ancestral ceremonies did not fall exclusively on the eldest son; instead, all the children took turns, which also meant that women could receive an inheritance so that they could finance the ceremonies. Divorce was not as

strictly taboo as it became in the fully Confucianized society, and remarriage was permitted in earlier Korean society.

19. Zhao Tingyang, *All Under Heaven: The Tianxia System for Possible World Order*, trans. Joseph E. Harroff (Oakland: University of California Press, 2021), 22–23.

20. "A Love Song For Latasha: ALWH & Netflix Screening & Conversation for Black Girls" (2021), https://www.youtube.com/watch?v=hRnLCKJyaAY, 23:41–23:45.

21. I developed the idea of "narrative philosophy" in my discussion of the Korean Buddhist nun and thinker Kim Iryŏp, whom I also mention in this book. In *Women and Buddhist Philosophy* (2016), I argued that Iryŏp's approach to philosophy—drawing materials from her personal life stories and integrating them with Buddhist philosophy, as well as doing philosophy through her own life experiences—could be defined as narrative philosophy. I contrasted this approach with Western, male-dominated, and theory-based philosophy.

22. Jay Caspian Kang, *The Loneliest Americans* (New York: Crown, 2022), 65.

5. Reflexive Engagement

1. Gi-Wook Shin, a sociologist, said, "Anti-Americanism became a new form of nationalism that fueled Korea's march for democracy" in the 1980s. Gi-Wook Shin and Kyung Moon Hwang, eds. *Contentious Kwangju: The May 18 Uprising in Korea's Past and Present* (Lanham, MD: Rowman & Littlefield, 2003), xxv.

2. Franz Fanon, *The Wretched of the Earth* (New York: Grove Press, 1963), 41.

3. Fanon, *The Wretched of the Earth*, 94.

4. Fanon, *The Wretched of the Earth*, 93.

5. Fanon, *The Wretched of the Earth*, 86.

6. Fanon, *The Wretched of the Earth*, 316.

7. Fanon, *The Wretched of the Earth*, 313.

8. Cho Sei-Hui, *Nanjangi ka ssoaollin chakŭn kong* (Seoul: Munhak kwa chisŏngsa, 1978), 340. Translation mine.

9. Dale S. Wright, *The Six Perfections: Buddhism and the Cultivation of Character* (New York: Oxford University Press, 2009), 3.
10. Jung Young Lee, *Marginality: The Key to Multicultural Theology* (Minneapolis: Fortress Press, 1995), 86.
11. Lee, *Marginality*, 80.
12. Chizuko Ueno, *Nationalism and Gender*, trans. Beverley Yamamoto (Melbourne: Trans Pacific Press, 2006), 178.
13. Ueno, *Nationalism and Gender*, 178.
14. Lama Rod Owens, "The Dharma of Trauma: Blackness, Buddhism, and Transhistorical Trauma Narrated Through Three Ayahusaca Ceremonies," *Black & Buddhist: What Buddhism Can Teach Us About Race, Resilience, Transformation & Freedom*, ed., Pamela Ayo Yetunde and Cheryl A. Giles (Boston: Shambhala, 2020), 52.
15. Kim Suyŏng, "P'urŭn hanŭl," in *Kim Suyŏng shijip kŏdaehan ppuri* (Seoul: Minŭmsa, 1978), 73. Translation mine.
16. Kim Iryŏp, "In'gyŏk ch'angjoe—kwagŏ ilgaenyŏnŭl hoesang hayŏ," *Sinyŏsŏng* (August 1924). Reprinted in Kim Iryŏp, *Kkot i chimyŏn nun i siryŏra* (Seoul: Osangsa, 1985), 87. Translation mine.
17. Kim Suyŏng, "P'ul," in *Kim Suyŏng shijip kŏdaehan ppuri*, 154. Translation mine.
18. Tanabe Hajime, *Philosophy as Metanoetics*, trans. Takeuchi Yoshinori (Berkeley: University of California Press, 1986), 66.
19. Rima Vesely-Flad, *Black Buddhists and the Black Radical Tradition: The Practice of Stillness in the Movement for Liberation* (New York: New York University Press, 2022), 1.
20. Vesely-Flad, *Black Buddhists and the Black Radical Tradition*, 2.

Epilogue

1. Julian Mark, Taylor Telford, and Susan Svrluga, "In First Days, Trump Deals 'Death Blow' to DEI and Affirmative Action," *Washington Post*, January 23, 2025.
2. Jeremy B. Merrill, Azi Paybarah, and Eric Lau, "How Federal Agencies Have Already Changed Their Websites Under Trump," *Washington Post*, January 31, 2025.

3. David E. Sanger, "Trump Blames D.E.I. and Biden for Crash Under His Watch," *New York Times*, January 30, 2025.

4. McKinsey & Company has produced a series of reports including: "Diversity Wins: How Inclusion Matters" (2020), "Race in the Workplace: The Black Experience" (2021), "Diversity Wins" (2021), and "The State Of Diversity in Global Private Markets: 2023."

5. A report from the *Wall Street Journal* shows that DEI has had only limited impact on workforce composition. Inti Pacheco, Elizaveta Galkina, and Theo Francis, "DEI Didn't Change the Workforce All That Much. A Look at 13 Million Jobs," *Wall Street Journal*, February 7, 2025.

6. Liz Elting, "Why Corporate America Should Reconsider Scaling Back DEI," *Forbes*, November 11, 2024.

7. "Census Bureau Releases New Educational Attainment Data," United States Census Bureau, February 16, 2023, https://www.census.gov/newsroom/press-releases/2023/educational-attainment-data.html.

8. "Education Pays, 2022," *Career Outlook*, US Bureau of Labor Statistics, May 2023, https://www.bls.gov/careeroutlook/2023/data-on-display/education-pays.htm.

9. "Education Pays, 2022," *Career Outlook*.

10. José Medina, *The Epistemology of Protest; Silencing, Epistemic Activism, and the Communicative Life of Resistance* (Oxford: Oxford University Press, 2023), 6. Italics in the original.

11. Medina, *The Epistemology of Protest*, 7.

Index

Abelmann, Nancy, 94–95
academic philosophy, 25–29, 35.
    See also philosophy
activism, 4, 135; epistemic, 150
affirmative action, 6, 146
African Americans: Black-Korean
    conflict, 87–96, 107–10;
    introduction to, 6; marginality
    of, 31–32, 113, 132–33; slavery, 12,
    19, 36–39, 41, 76–80, 109; social
    invisibility of, 11–12. *See also*
    Black Americans; minority
    against minority
Allison, Sophia Nahli, 110–11
American Association of University
    Professors, 46
American Dream, 90, 93, 95, 98
Anderson, Benedict, 23–24, 154n14
Anglo-American culture, 36, 89
anti-American sentiment, 115–16
anti-Semitism, 29, 54

Aoki, Guy, 99
April Revolution (1960), 135
Arendt, Hannah: on Eichmann,
    19–20; on power, 28–29
artificial intelligence (AI), 39–40
Art of War, The (Sun Tzu), 116
Asian Americans: formation of the
    identity of, 112–14; invisibility of,
    10–12, 91, 103; Vincent Chen and,
    112. *See also* Chinese Americans;
    Japanese Americans; Korean
    Americans
Asian woman identity, 64, 149
asylum seekers, 22–23, 38, 73–74
atmosphere of violence, 66
autonomy, 83–84, 137–38

Baldwin, James, 31–32, 57
Benjamin, Walter: on divine
    violence, 71–72
bias, 35–36, 65, 123–24, 128

INDEX

167

INDEX

GPSR Authorized Representative: Easy Access System Europe, Mustamäe tee 50, 10621 Tallinn, Estonia, gpsr.requests@easproject.com